WITHDRAWN

Insight Study Guide
Theo Hummer

The Scarlet Letter

Nathaniel Hawthorne

insight

insight

Nathaniel Hawthorne's The Scarlet Letter by Theo Hummer
Insight Study Guide series

Copyright © 2011 Insight Publications Pty Ltd

First published in 2011 by
Insight Publications Pty Ltd
ABN 57 005 102 983
89 Wellington Street
St Kilda VIC 3182
Australia
Tel: +61 3 9523 0044
Fax: +61 3 9523 2044
Email: books@insightpublications.com
Website: www.insightpublications.com

This edition published in 2011 in the United States of America by
Insight Publications Pty Ltd, Australia.

ISBN-13: 978-1-921411-85-4

Library of Congress Control Number: 2011931353

Cover Design by The Modern Art Production Group
Cover Illustrations by The Modern Art Production Group,
istockphoto* and House Industries
Internal Design by Sarn Potter

Printed in the United States of America by Lightning Source
10 9 8 7 6 5 4 3 2 1

contents

CHARACTER MAP

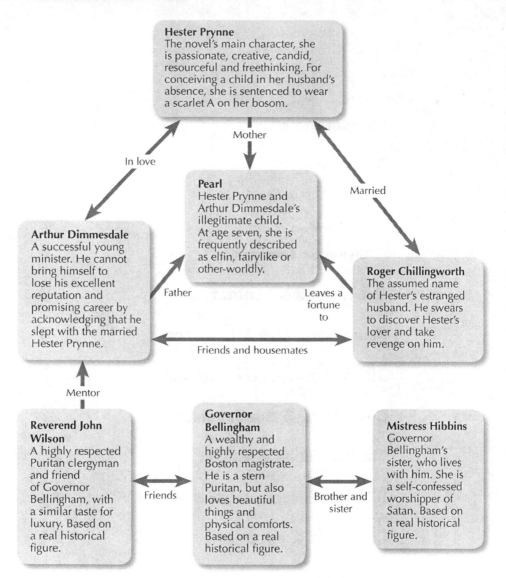

Hester Prynne
The novel's main character, she is passionate, creative, candid, resourceful and freethinking. For conceiving a child in her husband's absence, she is sentenced to wear a scarlet A on her bosom.

In love

Mother

Married

Pearl
Hester Prynne and Arthur Dimmesdale's illegitimate child. At age seven, she is frequently described as elfin, fairylike or other-worldly.

Arthur Dimmesdale
A successful young minister. He cannot bring himself to lose his excellent reputation and promising career by acknowledging that he slept with the married Hester Prynne.

Father

Leaves a fortune to

Roger Chillingworth
The assumed name of Hester's estranged husband. He swears to discover Hester's lover and take revenge on him.

Friends and housemates

Mentor

Reverend John Wilson
A highly respected Puritan clergyman and friend of Governor Bellingham, with a similar taste for luxury. Based on a real historical figure.

Friends

Governor Bellingham
A wealthy and highly respected Boston magistrate. He is a stern Puritan, but also loves beautiful things and physical comforts. Based on a real historical figure.

Brother and sister

Mistress Hibbins
Governor Bellingham's sister, who lives with him. She is a self-confessed worshipper of Satan. Based on a real historical figure.

The Puritans of Boston
Dour, judgemental and always gossiping, but with a capacity for kindness. The people of Boston represent prevailing attitudes and normative (mainstream, authorised) values.

OVERVIEW

About the author

Nathaniel Hawthorne was born in 1804 to Nathaniel Hathorne [sic] and Elizabeth Manning. His father, a ship's captain, died in 1808. Nathaniel Senior's family, the Hathornes, though not wealthy, were an old Salem family who considered themselves socially far superior to Elizabeth's family, the Mannings. After Nathaniel Senior's death, Elizabeth and her son went back to the Mannings' home, where Hawthorne grew up. After his education at Bowdoin College in Maine in the early 1820s, Hawthorne returned to the Mannings in Salem to hone his writing skills. During this time, while studying New England history, he learned about his Hathorne ancestors' role in the Salem witch trials of the 1690s. It was 'perhaps as a gesture of separation from these judgemental people who had hanged witches and wanted nothing to do with his mother and himself' (p.ix) that he changed the spelling of his name to Hawthorne.

Hawthorne's first book, a collection of short stories called *Twice-Told Tales*, was published in 1837. It didn't sell especially well, but critics liked it. One enthusiastic supporter – the educator, reformer and transcendentalist Elizabeth Peabody – introduced Hawthorne to her sister Sophia, whom Hawthorne would marry. Hawthorne lived briefly at the utopian commune, Brook Farm, and moved, after his marriage, to Concord, where he was friends with transcendentalists such as Ralph Waldo Emerson, Henry David Thoreau and Margaret Fuller. Though Hawthorne wasn't a transcendentalist himself, he found them to be stimulating company. He shared with them a Romantic world view, valuing individuality, emotion and nature over tradition, rationalism and technological progress. He published another book of short stories, *Mosses from an Old Manse*, in 1846.

Also in 1846, Hawthorne had to bow to financial concerns. In order to support his young family, he reluctantly agreed to take advantage of the political spoils system of the day and accept the surveyorship of the Custom House at the Salem harbour. This job involved very few responsibilities; despite (or perhaps because of) that, Hawthorne found it numbing and was unable to complete writing another manuscript until after the election of 1848, which left his Democrat patrons out of office and Hawthorne out of a job. To add to his misfortunes, Hawthorne also lost his beloved mother in 1849.

Still, the period that followed was a prolific one for Hawthorne. He published *The Scarlet Letter* in 1850, *The House of the Seven Gables* in 1851 and *The Blithedale Romance* in 1852. Hawthorne moved back to Concord to enjoy the company of his transcendentalist friends and made a new writer friend, Herman Melville. In 1853, he was appointed American Consul in Liverpool, England; but again, office work interfered with his creativity. He held this job until 1857, then lived in Italy until 1859. Upon returning to the US, he published his last novel, *The Marble Faun* (1860). His ill health and the changing literary tastes of Americans probably both contributed to his inability to finish any more of the novels he began writing. Hawthorne died in 1864, having never achieved his goal of writing a bestseller, but the importance of his powerful, quintessentially American writing continues to grow.

Synopsis

The Scarlet Letter begins with a long preface – 'The Custom-House' – in which Hawthorne blends autobiography and fiction to show both the historical distance and the close connections between himself (writing in the late 1840s) and the action of the novel (set in the 1640s). 'The Custom-House' sets up Hawthorne's preference for creativity and human connection over decorum and career ambitions; these values are at the heart of *The Scarlet Letter*.

The novel proper begins in 1642, as Hester Prynne mounts the scaffold at the centre of Boston, wearing on her bosom, for the first time, the embroidered A that marks her as a convicted adulteress. The scarlet A seems superfluous: Boston in 1642 is a small enough town for everyone to know that Hester has recently given birth to a baby girl (Pearl) despite the fact that she has been in Boston for two years and her husband has not yet arrived from England to join her. Thus, the scarlet letter of shame exists not only as an embroidered badge, but also as a mark of town gossip and as a symbol embodied in the child born out of wedlock.

Adultery requires two parties, but Hester bears her punishment alone. She is determined to protect her lover from disgrace and refuses to reveal his name. Hester's husband arrives in Boston just in time to witness her shame. He asks her not to reveal his identity either. He prefers not to be known as a cuckold (a husband who has been cheated on) and, besides, he has decided that he will secretly discover and take revenge on Hester's lover. He takes the name Roger Chillingworth and introduces himself in Boston as a physician.

As time goes on, we become increasingly aware that Pearl's father must be Arthur Dimmesdale, a scholarly young minister with a gift for oratory and a saintly reputation. Dimmesdale becomes sick and, eventually, Chillingworth moves in with him as his doctor and supposed friend. Meanwhile, Hester takes a cottage on the edge of town. She accepts her lot as an outcast, yet takes every opportunity to help people who are in trouble. Hester supports herself by doing fancy needlework; there's more of a market for such ornate objects than you would expect in an austere Puritan colony. She also creates whimsical, fantastically beautiful clothes for Pearl. Pearl is obsessed with questions about the scarlet letter Hester wears on her bosom; these questions cause Hester pain. In Boston, the significance of the letter has begun to shift: people remember that it originally stood for 'adulteress', but the many whom Hester has aided whisper that it stands instead for 'able'. Only Pearl seems to think that the letter is connected to Arthur Dimmesdale's habit of clutching his heart in pain.

The novel builds towards two dramatic tableaux that both occur in 1649 on the same scaffold where Hester was shamed in 1642. The first occurs on the night of Governor John Winthrop's death. Hounded by guilt, Arthur Dimmesdale decides to spend the night standing on the scaffold. As it happens, Hester and Pearl encounter him there and he asks them to join him. Since it's the middle of the night, Dimmesdale's gesture of confession is secret and fairly pointless. However, as they stand there, the night sky is lit up by a comet that seems to leave a scarlet A in the sky.

Dimmesdale is certain that this is the mark of God's judgement against him, but people around Boston say that the A stands for 'angel' and marks the death of the beloved governor. Pearl challenges Dimmesdale to acknowledge her and her mother in daylight as he does in the secrecy of night, but Dimmesdale does not meet that challenge until the climax of the novel.

The climactic tableau occurs after Hester and Dimmesdale have agreed that they will leave Boston and begin a new life together. Their departure date coincides with the day that Dimmesdale delivers the Election Day sermon, the crowning achievement of his brilliant young career. After his triumphant sermon, his health fails dramatically. He has Hester assist him onto the scaffold of the pillory and, there, he bares his chest – which may or may not be branded with a letter A matching Hester's – to the crowd, then joins hands with Hester and Pearl, and dies. (His mission of revenge complete, Chillingworth soon dies too.) Dimmesdale never feels redeemed for his affair with Hester; his life has been one of hypocrisy. Hester, by contrast, ends life many years later, regarded by Bostonians as a beloved advisor. She has been publicly marked by shame and sin, yet her kindness and honesty make her strong. She seems to be at peace.

Character summaries

Hester Prynne: The novel's main character. In the absence of her much older husband, Roger Chillingworth, she falls in love with Arthur Dimmesdale and gives birth to Pearl. As punishment for this adultery she must wear the scarlet letter A on her clothes. She makes her living doing fancy needlework.

Pearl: The illegitimate daughter of Hester Prynne and Arthur Dimmesdale. As a child, she tends to be emotionally reserved and frequently hurts her mother's feelings without meaning to, but after the emotional scene of Arthur Dimmesdale's death at the end of the book she becomes warmer and kinder.

Arthur Dimmesdale: A successful young religious minister, lover of Hester and father of Pearl. He spends most of the novel tormenting himself with secret penances, public hypocrisy and fantasies about the importance to everyone in Boston of his sin and confession.

Roger Chillingworth: The assumed name of Hester's older husband. When he arrives in Boston and discovers that Hester has betrayed him, he decides to keep his true identity a secret, and to discover Hester's lover and take revenge.

Governor Bellingham: A wealthy and highly respected magistrate, he represents Puritan Boston's legal power structure. He and the other magistrates are slower than the ordinary people of Boston to forgive Hester Prynne.

Mistress Hibbins: Governor Bellingham's sister, who lives with him. Mistress Hibbins may be insane. She talks openly about meeting with Satan, but faces no legal punishments – just a bad reputation.

Reverend John Wilson: A highly respected Puritan clergyman and friend of Governor Bellingham, with a similar taste for luxury. He is Arthur Dimmesdale's spiritual and professional mentor.

The Puritans of Boston: The people of Boston function like a Greek chorus, indicating prevailing attitudes. Their changing views of Hester Prynne – from scorn and disgust at the novel's beginning to love and respect at its end – reflect Hester's changing views of herself and possibly the progress of her relationship with God as she works to make up for her sin.

BACKGROUND & CONTEXT

The American Renaissance

In the 1840s and 1850s, US writers were busy producing some of nineteenth-century America's most important works of literature: Ralph Waldo Emerson's *Essays* (1841 and 1844), Frederick Douglass' *Narrative of the Life of Frederick Douglass, an American Slave* (1845), Emily Dickinson's poems (most not published until after her death, but written from around 1850), Nathaniel Hawthorne's *The Scarlet Letter* (1850) and *The House of the Seven Gables* (1851), Herman Melville's *Moby-Dick* (1851), Harriet Beecher Stowe's *Uncle Tom's Cabin* (1852), Henry David Thoreau's *Walden* (1854) and Walt Whitman's first edition of *Leaves of Grass* (1855). This outpouring of literary works was centred mainly in New England and the period during which it occurred is sometimes also called American Romanticism because it marked a departure from tradition and rationalism, and turned towards humanism and emotion. It celebrated nature and spirituality rather than technological progress and organised religion, and it supported democratic inclusivity and a brand of individualism that never turned its back on civic responsibility.

The American Renaissance was very much concerned with questions of what it meant to be American; hence Hawthorne's ongoing fascination with his Puritan heritage, seen in stories such as 'The Minister's Black Veil' and 'Young Goodman Brown' as well as in *The Scarlet Letter*, even as he repudiated many Puritan values. American Renaissance writers tended to be politically engaged but somewhat hard to classify: most of them opposed slavery, as did the Whig party of their day, but they also tended to oppose bureaucracy and the growth of capitalism, as did the Democratic party of their day. The American Renaissance ended as the country began to tear apart with the approach of the Civil War.

Puritan New England

Although the Puritans were an offshoot of the Church of England, their theology and practices were much closer to those of the Scottish Calvinists. Their beliefs and practices included: extreme simplicity of worship; opposition to many secular pastimes, such as card-playing and maypole-dancing, and to the celebration of many traditional Christian holidays, such as Christmas; belief in original sin and natural depravity, that is, that humans are born bad and must depend upon divine grace for salvation; and the belief that God has foreordained everything that will happen, including who is elect (destined to be saved on Judgement Day) and who is reprobate (destined not to be saved). The most extreme Puritans were those who left England first for the Netherlands and then for New England, where they founded a theocracy. The same Governor John Winthrop whose death is remarked upon in Chapter 12 of *The Scarlet Letter* preached a sermon in 1630 that called for New England to consider itself 'a city upon a hill', that is, an example for the rest of the world, as Jesus exhorted his followers to be in Matthew 5:14. By the 1680s, the Puritans' intolerance of other Christian sects, especially the Quakers, began to provoke England into intervening in the Puritans' governance of New England. In 1689, a broad religious tolerance act effectively put an end to Puritan rule in what was still an English colony.

Hawthorne plays pretty fast and loose with his representation of Puritans. In many ways, his characters' interests, obsessions and repressions seem more like those of his uptight Victorian contemporaries than of his Puritan ancestors. This lack of historical accuracy allows him to explore the themes that he wants to explore and is a big part of why he calls his book a 'romance', not a 'novel'.

GENRE, STRUCTURE & LANGUAGE

Genre

The romance vs the novel

In the twentieth and twenty-first centuries, the term **novel** has been used for any book-length work of fiction. However, Hawthorne recognised two varieties of book-length fiction: the **novel** and the **romance**. Hawthorne saw himself as a writer of romances.

In his preface to *The House of Seven Gables*, Hawthorne explains that novels stick closely 'not merely to the possible, but to the probable and ordinary course of man's experience' (1851, p.v), indicating that his idea of the novel is similar to our idea of realist fiction. Romances, on the other hand, are more concerned with 'the truth of the human heart' (1851, p.v), so they are free to create fantastic situations and larger-than-life characters, and to 'bring out or mellow the lights and deepen and enrich the shadows of [their] picture[s]' (1851, p.v). Emotional truth is the focus. Romances can employ symbols and impressionistic descriptions; they can include magical or supernatural elements; they depict the world not as we rationally know it to be, but as we – emotional, biased creatures that we are – experience it.

Hawthorne's description in 'The Custom-House' of moonlight's power to inspire the imagination can help us to understand his aims in creating *The Scarlet Letter* not as a novel, but as a romance. He tells us that the objects of our ordinary experience are 'spiritualized' by moonlight (p.35). Things that are familiar and practical in daylight become 'invested with a quality of strangeness and remoteness' (p.35). Like a moonlit room, the romance genre as Hawthorne practised it is 'a neutral territory, somewhere between the real world and fairy-land, where the Actual and the Imaginary may meet, and each imbue itself with the nature of the other' (p.35).

Hawthorne populates *The Scarlet Letter* with Puritans from New England's real history, but he uses those Puritans more to represent his ideas about rigid religious and moral doctrine than to show us what Puritan life was really like. He also creates a world in which the miraculous appearance of letters in the sky or on Arthur Dimmesdale's flesh seem possible, and in which little Pearl's inherent goodness and wildness can tame and attract wild animals. The external, physical world of *The Scarlet Letter* reflects the internal, emotional worlds of its characters – both the individual emotional struggles of Hester Prynne and Arthur Dimmesdale, and the collective attitudes of the Puritans of Boston.

Twentieth- and twenty-first-century inheritors of the romance tradition include psychological fiction and magic realism.

Structure

Frame narrative

In a **frame narrative**, the main events are presented as a story within a story. For example, in Emily Brontë's 1847 novel *Wuthering Heights*, the main story of Catherine and Heathcliff is related to Mr Lockwood by his housekeeper, Ellen Dean. We are introduced to Mr Lockwood at the beginning of the novel, we discover the main story alongside him, and we return to his world and his viewpoint at the novel's end. Mr Lockwood is not a particularly interesting character in and of himself, but his world provides an occasion for the telling of the main story as well as perspectives on it. The frame structure also creates distance between the author and narrator, casting some doubt on the main story's accuracy: we can trust Emily Brontë but still wonder whether Ellen Dean is embellishing the facts. Finally, our return to the framing perspective at the novel's end provides closure and an opportunity for reflection.

By beginning *The Scarlet Letter* with the preface 'The Custom-House', in which he describes his own relationship to the New England Puritans and relates the (fictional) story of how the novel's main events came to his attention, Hawthorne provides an opening frame for his romance. However, he never closes this frame. At the book's end, we do not return to Hawthorne or the Salem customs house. The final chapter shifts forward in time to relate the events of the second half or so of Hester Prynne's life, but it doesn't return to the nineteenth-century perspective of 'The Custom-House'. This unclosed frame leaves the door open between the reader's world and the world of the main story; it is as if Hester, Dimmesdale and Pearl continue to haunt us after the end of the book.

The meaning of the letter

'What does the letter mean, mother?' little Pearl asks (p.158). This question recurs so often that it seems a reader who discovers the meaning of the scarlet letter will also know the meaning of *The Scarlet Letter*. The novel addresses a central question: How certain can we be of what a symbol means? The Puritan magistrates sentence Hester to wear the scarlet letter as a mark of her shameful crime: 'A' for adulteress. However, from the moment we are introduced to the letter, it is already working to undercut and undo that meaning:

> 'It was so artistically done, and with so much fertility and gorgeous luxuriance of fancy, that it had all the effect of a last and fitting decoration to the apparel which she wore' (p.50).

Is the scarlet letter, then, a mark of shame or an ornament?

The people of Boston are convinced at the novel's beginning that Hester is a criminal and that the A is her brand of shame, but Hester's good works begin to unsettle that interpretation:

> 'She was self-ordained a Sister of Mercy ... The letter was the symbol of her calling ... They said that it meant Able; so strong was Hester Prynne, with a woman's strength' (p.141).

On the night of Governor John Winthrop's death, a scarlet letter, which the Bostonians 'interpret to stand for Angel' (p.138), appears in the sky. If Governor Winthrop's scarlet A marks him as an angel, then how are we to read Hester Prynne's? Could it be A for Arthur, solving the public mystery of who Pearl's father is? A for Adam and his apple, the sources of original sin? A for America? The letter's uncertain and shifting significance introduces a broader thread of uncertainty to the novel and ultimately implies that there may be no authority who can fix meanings or guarantee absolute truth.

Language

'Thee' and 'thou'

Characters in *The Scarlet Letter* address each other as **thee** and **thou** a lot. To twenty-first-century ears, these pronouns sound archaic. We probably know them only from the works of William Shakespeare or the King James Bible, which means that most of the time when we hear them, we're all dressed up and on our best behaviour. For these reasons, they may sound formal to us, but for the characters in *The Scarlet Letter*, these pronouns would actually have been more intimate and casual than the 'you' we are used to. If you have studied a foreign language, you have probably come across a similar distinction somewhere along the way – the English you/thou distinction fits perfectly with the French *vous/tu*. 'Thee' and 'thou' are second-person singular pronouns that were used with children, family members and close friends, while 'you' was reserved for second-person plural and more formal relationships. Grammatically, 'thou' was used as a subject (as 'I' is in the first person) and 'thee' was used as an object (as 'me' is in the first person).

CHAPTER-BY-CHAPTER ANALYSIS

'The Custom-House – Introductory' (pp.7–43)

Summary: *Nathaniel Hawthorne discovers the scarlet letter in the attic of the customs house in Salem, Massachusetts.*

'The Custom-House' can be frustratingly dry for first-time readers of *The Scarlet Letter*, but it is still worth paying attention to. It serves as a framing device that allows Hawthorne to pretend that *The Scarlet Letter* is a true story that he is retelling, not making up. By 1850, such a device was already a longstanding convention for novels. Hawthorne's descriptions of his family's Puritan roots in Salem and of his numbing work in the customs house there *are* true, and these descriptions set up the central conflicts of the novel: between authority, tradition, self-congratulation and careerism on the one hand and individuality, idealism, passion and creativity on the other.

Hawthorne begins 'The Custom-House' by describing his mixed feelings about Salem. Although he feels deeply connected to the birthplace and final resting place of generations of his ancestors, Hawthorne imagines those same ancestors disapproving of him as a 'degenerate' and mere 'writer of storybooks' (p.13). In addition to describing how work as a customs house surveyor deadened his creativity, Hawthorne provides portraits of his colleagues that range from gently mocking – the Collector, a 'gallant old General' (p.21) – to scathing – the 'permanent Inspector', a man 'with no higher moral responsibilities than the beasts of the field' (p.20). Hawthorne tells us that his colleagues belong mainly to the Whig political party (p.16); the party of economic and bureaucratic modernisation, of big urban business. Hawthorne was himself a Democrat, committed to a more traditional agrarian economy in which people were closely tied to the physical means of their support. In claiming that bureaucratic work dehumanises people, 'The Custom-House' anticipates Hawthorne's friend Herman Melville's 1853 story, 'Bartleby the Scrivener'.

'The Custom-House' builds towards two lyrical passages near its end. Both emphasise Hawthorne's Romantic sensibility. In one, Hawthorne sings the praises of moonlight, which shows familiar objects 'almost as vividly … as by daylight' but 'now invested with a quality of strangeness' that awakens and inspires the imagination (p.35). In the other – the key scene of 'The Custom-House' – Hawthorne finds Hester Prynne's ornately embroidered scarlet A in the customs house attic and lays it on his own chest (p.32). With this gesture, Hawthorne connects himself to his heroine, Hester Prynne: their passion and nonconformity mark them both as outsiders.

Q Hawthorne describes two of his ancestors as 'stern and black-browed Puritans' who would consider his literary ambitions and achievements 'worthless, if not positively disgraceful', yet he also admits that 'strong traits of their nature have intertwined themselves with mine' (p.13). What is Hawthorne telling us about the society in which the rest of *The Scarlet Letter* is set?

Chapters 1 and 2: 'The Prison-Door' and 'The Market-Place' (pp.45–55)

Summary: *We meet Hester Prynne as she is led from the prison to the scaffold.*

In 'The Prison-Door,' Hawthorne presents Boston's Puritans in their black and grey clothes, and associates them with their cemetery and their heavy, ugly prison. In contrast, he shows us 'a wild rose-bush, covered … with its delicate gems' (p.45) growing at the very door of the prison. He connects this rose bush with Anne Hutchinson, a woman famously banished from Massachusetts in 1638 for disagreeing with Puritan leaders.

In 'The Market-Place', we begin by listening to the gossiping crowd that waits to watch Hester Prynne stand on the scaffold of the town pillory in a spectacle of guilt. We learn that the citizens of Boston deeply disapprove of Hester and her crime – adultery – though they are too solemn and earnest to mock her. Then, Hester emerges from the prison door. Like the rose bush in the previous chapter, she is much more beautiful than her surroundings, but her beauty is mixed with shame. Richly embroidered on the bosom of her dress is the letter A, which brands her as an adulteress. In her arms is a three-month-old baby. The letter and the baby are linked: each is a 'token of her shame' (p.50). Near the end of the chapter, Hester's memories reveal that she was born in England and married there to a 'misshapen scholar' (p.55) much older than herself.

Q Why would the Puritans consider it a punishment for Hester to stand on a platform and be the centre of attention?

Q What is Hawthorne telling us about Hester by having her create and wear such a 'wild and picturesque' gown (p.51) for the occasion of her public shaming?

Key vocabulary
Heterodox: Differing from authorised teachings; unorthodox.
Magistrate: A judge. The word is sometimes used more generally to refer to any high government authority.
Pillory: Like stocks or a whipping post, a structure used to immobilise a condemned criminal either for public humiliation or while being beaten.
Scaffold: A raised public structure on which punishments were performed.

Chapters 3 and 4: 'The Recognition' and 'The Interview' (pp.56–70)

Summary: We meet Arthur Dimmesdale and Roger Chillingworth.

Although we aren't introduced to Roger Chillingworth by name until 'The Interview', Hester notices him at the edge of the crowd at the beginning of 'The Recognition'. He and Hester make eye contact, but Chillingworth 'raised his finger … and laid it on his lips' (p.57) as a sign that Hester should not identify him as her husband. This is the chapter's first and more obvious 'recognition'.

Most of the chapter, though, is devoted to Hester and Arthur Dimmesdale's mutual recognition that neither of them plans to reveal that he is the father of her child. Calling this a 'recognition' is ironic since it conceals rather than reveals Hester's lover's identity. Ironies pile up in 'The Recognition' as Hester's minister, who is also Dimmesdale, publicly urges her to name her partner in shame even as he is privately relieved that she doesn't. Although the crowd cannot do so, we readers recognise that Dimmesdale is a coward who blames even his own hypocrisy on Hester.

The ironies continue in 'The Interview' when Chillingworth visits Hester in her prison cell. Although he is 'the man whom she had most deeply and irreparably injured' (p.68), he offers soothing medicine to both Hester and her baby. He asks that Hester not reveal that he is her husband; both of them note the parallel between this secret and the secret of her lover's identity. Chillingworth acknowledges that by marrying Hester even though he knew she didn't love him, he wronged her as much as she has since wronged him. 'But, Hester, the man lives who has wronged us both' (p.69), he says. Chillingworth vows to discover Hester's lover and take revenge, not by killing or publicly shaming him, but in some other, secret way. The stage is set for a triangular drama. Chillingworth declares:

> 'I find here a woman, a man, a child, amongst whom and myself there exist the closest ligaments. No matter whether of love or of hate' (p.70).

Q At the end of the chapter (p.70), Hester asks Chillingworth whether, like the devil, he has 'enticed me into a bond that will prove the ruin of my soul?' and Chillingworth responds, 'No, not thine!' Whose soul does Chillingworth imply will be ruined – Dimmesdale's or his own? Why do you think so?

Chapters 5 and 6: 'Hester at Her Needle' and 'Pearl' (pp.71–88)

Summary: Released from jail, Hester and her daughter Pearl move to the edge of town.

Hester decides not to leave Boston and start life anew elsewhere, partly because she prefers to stay near Dimmesdale (although she fears that in continuing to care for him, she renews her sin) and partly because she feels that she must remain and suffer there in order to be redeemed. She moves into an abandoned cottage at the edge of town and makes a good living by doing fancy embroidery; even though the Puritans dress plainly most of the time, they still need ornamented clothes for special occasions.

In all of her interactions with people, Hester is conscious that they see her as a living embodiment of sin. Moreover, her own sin and repentance (or, perhaps, the mystical power of the scarlet letter) make her particularly sensitive and empathetic to others' sins. She is keenly aware that although she is the only one marked, the supposedly pure people around her are also all sinners. However, she tries to suppress this knowledge in order to keep her repentance and her idealism alive.

As her baby was conceived in sin, Hester is afraid that her daughter, Pearl, will prove to be somehow bad. However, the little girl, though passionate and unruly like her mother, grows more beautiful and intelligent with each passing day, and Hester considers her a treasure and dresses her richly. Pearl is as unaccepted by the Puritan children as her mother is by the Puritan adults, but Pearl's elfish and unearthly loveliness seem to imply that good can sometimes come from evil, that sin need not breed sin. Pearl is fascinated with Hester's scarlet letter and often unwittingly reminds Hester of her sin and pain by calling attention to the mark of shame. Amidst ugly neighbourhood rumours that Pearl is a demon's child and Pearl's own impish pranks, Hester is constantly worried that she has passed her sin on to her child.

Q What is the significance of the repeated associations between Pearl and the scarlet letter?

Key vocabulary

Sumptuary laws: Laws that restricted spending on luxury goods, especially clothes and food, for people below a certain income. These laws reinforced the social class structure by making it visible: only rich people were allowed to wear lace, jewellery, etc.

Chapters 7 and 8: 'The Governor's Hall' and 'The Elf-Child and the Minister' (pp.89–103)

Summary: With the help of Arthur Dimmesdale, Hester convinces Governor Bellingham not to take Pearl away from her.

'The Governor's Hall' mainly focuses on lavish displays of beauty: the richly imaginative garments that Hester makes for Pearl and the gorgeous luxury in which Governor Bellingham lives. Pearl's beautiful clothing echoes the elaborately ornamented scarlet letter Hester wears as a badge of shame, thus marking both of them as outlaws. The Governor's rich house, however, implies hypocrisy among the Puritan leadership, as Hawthorne makes clear at the beginning of 'The Elf-Child and the Minister'. In the first paragraph of the chapter, Hawthorne contrasts the Governor's 'aspect, so rigid and severe' with 'the appliances of worldly enjoyment wherewith he had evidently done his utmost to surround himself' (p.96). Similarly, the Governor's friend, 'the venerable pastor, John Wilson, however stern he might show himself in the pulpit, or in his public reproof of … transgressions', had 'a long established and legitimate taste for all good and comfortable things' (p.96). Members of Boston's Puritan establishment, it seems, are as partial to sensual pleasures as Hester is, but only she is publicly punished and scorned for it.

In 'The Elf-Child and the Minister', Pearl and Dimmesdale come face to face for the first time and share a brief, tender moment. Hawthorne's claim that 'marks of childish preference, accorded spontaneously by a spiritual instinct, and therefore seeming to imply in us something truly worthy to be loved' (p.102) reflects the Romantic view of children as having a special access to spiritual truth, lost to adults through experience, education and responsibility.

Governor Bellingham wants to remove Pearl from Hester's care because he believes that the sinful mother may endanger her daughter's immortal soul by not giving her an adequately Christian, moral upbringing. Hester makes the argument, which Dimmesdale then seconds and elaborates upon, that God has wisely given Pearl to Hester both as a joy and as a reminder of her sin. Hester and Dimmesdale point out that Hester, who has experienced sin and its consequences at first hand, is especially qualified to teach Pearl to be virtuous. They also point out that responsibility for Pearl will, in turn, keep Hester motivated to be a good Christian. Bellingham is convinced; Hester is allowed to keep Pearl.

Q John Wilson says that as long as no one knows who Pearl's father is, 'every good Christian man hath a title to show a father's kindness towards the poor, deserted babe' (p.103). What does he mean by this? How do you think Hester feels about every good Christian man behaving as if he were her child's father?

Chapters 9 and 10: 'The Leech' and 'The Leech and His Patient' (pp.104–21)

Summary: Roger Chillingworth gets close to pale, sickly Arthur Dimmesdale.

Although the primary meaning of 'leech' in these chapter titles is 'doctor' (doctors in those days used leeches to relieve patients of the excess blood that was thought to cause an array of illnesses), a secondary meaning – 'sinister bloodsucker' – is definitely present. Dimmesdale's health has been failing and Dr Roger Chillingworth has taken a special interest in him. 'A man burdened with a secret should especially avoid the intimacy of his physician' (p.109), Hawthorne writes, 'and yet no secret, such as the physician fancied must exist there, ever stole out of the minister's consciousness into his companion's ear' (p.110). Still, Chillingworth has a strong suspicion that Dimmesdale is the man he is looking for, Hester's lover. They move into the same boarding house; here, Dimmesdale's room is decorated with tapestries depicting David and Bathsheba (an adulterous biblical couple who conceived a child while Bathsheba's husband was away), and Nathan the Prophet, who reprimanded David. Dimmesdale's reputation as a virtuous minister is growing and the more he tells people that he is a sinner, the more they see him as a saint. Meanwhile, rumour has it that Chillingworth may be the devil; he is becoming uglier as time goes by and people believe that this outer ugliness may reflect inner ugliness.

In 'The Leech and His Patient', Chillingworth and Dimmesdale debate whether it is better for a sinner to confess or to keep his secrets. While Chillingworth argues that secrets will manifest (show) themselves outwardly if not confessed, Dimmesdale comes up with one reason (or excuse) after another why a person might decide to keep his secrets, even though confessing would be a relief. Through a window, Chillingworth and Dimmesdale see Hester and Pearl walking in the graveyard; Chillingworth asks Dimmesdale whether Hester suffers less for having confessed her crime and Dimmesdale says he believes so. Finally, Chillingworth sneaks up on Dimmesdale while he is sleeping and looks at his bare chest, which Dimmesdale has, up to that point, kept hidden from him. We aren't told what Chillingworth sees there, but it provokes a response of 'wonder, joy, and horror' (p.121). We can only assume that Dimmesdale's inner sin has somehow marked his flesh.

Q What do you think of Roger Chillingworth's claim that 'a sickness, a sore place ... in your spirit' can show itself 'in your bodily frame' (p.119)? Do outward appearances always match inner truths?

Chapters 11 and 12: 'The Interior of a Heart' and 'The Minister's Vigil' (pp.122–138)

Summary: Dimmesdale is at the mercy of Chillingworth and his own cowardly hypocrisy.

Once Chillingworth is sure that Dimmesdale has a guilty secret, he becomes obsessed with emotionally torturing Dimmesdale, yet Dimmesdale doesn't realise Chillingworth is his enemy. Dimmesdale's misery lends power to his preaching. His burden of secret sin 'gave him sympathies so intimate with the sinful brotherhood of mankind; so that his heart ... sent its own throb of pain through a thousand other hearts, in gushes of sad, persuasive eloquence' (pp.124–25). From the pulpit, he confesses his sin, but only in vague terms:

> 'The minister well knew – subtle, but remorseful hypocrite that he was! – the light in which his vague confession would be viewed' (p.126).

His congregation thinks him saintlier all the time. Burdened by guilt, he fasts, deprives himself of sleep and scourges (whips) himself secretly.

One night, he decides to stand on the scaffold where Hester was punished. He fantasises about being caught there, convinced that anyone who saw him would immediately know his sin. He imagines that the revelation of his guilt would throw all of Boston into chaos:

> 'The whole tribe of decorous personages, who had never heretofore been seen with a single hair of their heads awry, would start into public view, with the disorder of a nightmare in their aspects' (pp.132–33).

As he stands on the platform, Dimmesdale sees Reverend Wilson, Governor Bellingham, Hester Prynne and Roger Chillingworth all coming home from caring for the dying Governor Winthrop. However, Dimmesdale is so absorbed in his own drama that he never asks himself whether he should have been there, too. He demands that Hester and Pearl climb the scaffold and hold his hands, but when Pearl asks him to act this scenario out publicly, he refuses. Finally, he 'extended his egotism over the whole expanse of nature' (p.136) by interpreting a meteor as a spectacular mark of his crime.

Q Hawthorne writes that Dimmesdale 'had spoken the very truth, and transformed it into the veriest falsehood' (p.126). How is this possible? What does Hawthorne mean? What is he saying about the relationship between the letter of the law (technical correctness) and the spirit of the law (purity of intention)?

Chapters 13 and 14: 'Another View of Hester' and 'Hester and the Physician' (pp.139–152)

Summary: *Hester Prynne gains a reputation for helpfulness; now the person who needs her help is Arthur Dimmesdale.*

'It is to the credit of human nature,' Hawthorne writes, 'that, except where its selfishness is brought into play, it loves more readily than it hates' (p.140). This may seem like faint praise, yet human forgetfulness has been kind to Hester in the seven years since Pearl's birth and her public shaming. She has lost her physical beauty, but she has earned the approval of the community on whose edge she lives. Hester is still tormented by shame. Though she feels she has no right to ask for the benefits of human connection, 'she was quick to acknowledge her sisterhood with the race of man' when she can help others (p.140). The community's leaders are slower to forgive Hester's sin, but most people in Boston now say that the embroidered A on her breast stands for Able (not Adulteress). There are also rumours that the letter provides supernatural protection from harm.

After meeting Dimmesdale at the scaffold, Hester realises that Chillingworth has been torturing him. Despite her promise seven years earlier, she decides that she is morally obligated to let Dimmesdale know that Chillingworth is her former husband. When she tells Chillingworth so, he does not object, but he also confesses that he cannot forgive Dimmesdale. Chillingworth now holds Dimmesdale (and Hester, though he forgives her) responsible not only for committing adultery, but also for changing him from a harmless scholar into a fiend obsessed with revenge.

Q Hester worries that Pearl's 'nature had something wrong in it, which continually betokened that she had been born amiss, – the effluence of her mother's lawless passion' (p.144). What is Hawthorne saying here about the relationship between a person's origin, her essence, or spirit, and her destiny?

Q Hester tells Chillingworth, 'Thou hast been deeply wronged, and hast it at thy will to pardon', but he says, 'I have no such power … it has all been a dark necessity … It is our fate' (p.152). Which character believes in free will and which believes in predestination? Which view is more likely to lead people to take responsibility for their actions, and why?

Chapters 15 and 16: 'Hester and Pearl' and 'A Forest Walk' (pp.153–164)

Summary: Pearl wonders what the scarlet letter means and why the minister keeps his hand over his heart.

Hawthorne gives us a sweet and playful account of imaginative little Pearl's seashore play. In her game of dress-up, she decorates herself with seaweed that is arranged to imitate her mother's A. When she rejoins her mother, Pearl fixates on the question of what Hester's scarlet letter means, 'as if the one only thing for which she had been sent into the world was to make out its hidden import' (p.155). Pearl even manages to connect Hester's letter with Dimmesdale's habit of holding his hand over his heart as if in pain, but Hester refuses to explain.

When they venture into the forest, where Hester hopes to encounter Dimmesdale and reveal Chillingworth's true identity, Pearl is still curious about the letter and wonders whether she will receive her own mark 'when I am a woman grown' (p.160). However, her latest obsession is with the Black Man, an early American pagan god or Christian devil. As Note 55 (pp.234–35) explains, this devil is not black-skinned, but black-clothed – ironically, like the Puritans themselves! Earlier in *The Scarlet Letter*, the Black Man was associated with Roger Chillingworth (e.g. p.70), but when Hester tells Pearl that, 'Once in my life I met the Black Man! ... This scarlet letter is his mark' (p.162), the Black Man seems to be Arthur Dimmesdale.

Q Chapters 14, 15 and 16 feature a great deal of Pearl playing by herself in natural settings – first the seashore, then the forest. How does Hawthorne represent nature? Is it beautiful or ugly, safe or dangerous, kindly or threatening or indifferent? Does Pearl seem to have a special relationship with nature? If so, what is that relationship like?

Chapters 17 and 18: 'The Pastor and His Parishioner' and 'A Flood of Sunshine' (pp.165–179)

Summary: Hester convinces Dimmesdale to leave Boston with her.

When Hester and Dimmesdale encounter each other in the gloomy forest, they seem to one another, at first, to be ghosts. Hester confesses that Chillingworth is her former husband; Dimmesdale is horrified and, at first, furious with her, but Hester insists that he forgive her. She reminds him that the world is big and Boston is the only place where their crime need ruin his life. Dimmesdale protests, 'I am powerless to go' (p.172), and he gives excuse after excuse, but Hester finds answers for all his doubts and fears. Finally, Dimmesdale admits that he is afraid to go alone. In assuring him that he need not go alone, Hester reveals to Dimmesdale that she still loves him.

When Dimmesdale finally agrees to leave Boston with Hester, sunshine breaks into the forest and changes the surroundings from gloomy to cheerful. Hester removes the scarlet A from her bosom and flings it onto the stream bank. Her beauty begins to return. She calls to Pearl, who has been playing in the forest. Hester hopes that Pearl and Dimmesdale will love one another, but Pearl seems wary of the minister.

Q 'The scarlet letter', Hawthorne writes, was Hester's 'passport into regions where other women dared not tread. Shame, Despair, Solitude! These had been her teachers, – stern and wild ones, – and they had made her strong, but taught her much amiss' (p.174). As Dimmesdale is a priest, on the other hand, 'the framework of his order inevitably hemmed him in … he might have been supposed safer within the line of virtue, than if he had never sinned at all' (p.175). What is Hawthorne saying about the relationship between order, respectability, virtue and freedom? Do you think Hawthorne really believes there is something 'amiss' in Hester's approach to the world?

Q The animals in the forest love Pearl: 'A wolf, it is said, – but here the tale has surely lapsed into the improbable, – came up …' (p.178). Hawthorne seems uncertain about whether or not the wolf really approached Pearl, but if he's the one making up the story, how can he not know? Within a fictional narrative, what is the difference between an event that really happened and one that is only rumoured to have happened? Why does Hawthorne create this uncertainty?

Key vocabulary

Estranged: Separated, physically but especially emotionally. Similar to *alienated*.

Malignity: Evil.

Chapters 19 and 20: 'The Child at the Brook-Side' and 'The Minister in a Maze' (pp.180–196)

Summary: Pearl doesn't warm up to Dimmesdale; nevertheless, Dimmesdale feels like a new man.

Hester and Dimmesdale remark upon Pearl's elfin beauty and her resemblance to them both. They beckon for her to join them, but she stands on the other side of the brook, refusing to approach; she even throws a temper tantrum. Finally, Hester realises that she must put the scarlet letter back on and put her loosened hair away. Once she has hidden her beauty and resumed her mark of shame, Pearl affectionately comes to her, but she still will not show any friendliness towards Dimmesdale. As she did on the scaffold, Pearl asks if Dimmesdale will walk hand in hand with her and her mother in public in Boston. When the answer is no, Pearl is not impressed. For Pearl, her mother's rejection of the scarlet letter is a rejection of her and she holds Hester accountable for that rejection, just as she holds Dimmesdale accountable for his refusal to acknowledge her.

When Dimmesdale returns to town, he feels a new vigour and has a series of mischievous impulses. He refuses medicine from Roger Chillingworth. At the same time, though, he is very pleased that he and Hester aren't planning to leave Boston until after he has given his special Election Day sermon. He stays up all night working on it with great enthusiasm.

Q When Dimmesdale returns to Boston, everything he sees has 'so very strange, and yet so familiar, an aspect … It was the same town as heretofore; but the same minister returned not from the forest' (p.189). Why does the change inside Dimmesdale make objects outside of him look different? What is Hawthorne showing us about human perception and the relationship between spiritual truth and physical appearances?

Chapters 21 and 22: 'The New England Holiday' and 'The Procession' (pp.197–214)

Summary: Election Day brings Hester bad news and renewed public shame.

Election Day in Boston is as close to a festive occasion as the Puritans of 1649 get. Everyone is out on the town square. Hawthorne notes that although the Puritans themselves are stern and strict, they don't mind the Native Americans' festive clothing or the outlandish costumes and public drinking of the Spanish crew of the ship that Hester has chosen for her voyage to England with Dimmesdale and Pearl. When he sees her on Election Day, the ship's captain tells Hester that Chillingworth, too, has booked passage on the ship – indicating, of course, that Chillingworth knows of their plan to escape and intends to pursue them.

When Dimmesdale appears to give his sermon, he looks healthier than he ever has. Pearl remarks upon this difference, once again noting scornfully his unwillingness to acknowledge her or her mother in public. Mistress Hibbins also remarks upon the change in Dimmesdale, in her longest speech of the whole book. Finally, people who have come to Boston from out of town watch Hester and her scarlet letter with such curiosity that it revives the curiosity even of the Bostonians, and the mark 'was thus made to sear her breast more painfully, than at any time since the first day she had put it on' (p.214). Hester, as the tormented sinner, and Dimmesdale, as Boston's local saint, are thus, on what they imagine to be their last day in Boston, fulfilling their accustomed roles in the community more perfectly than ever.

Q When Pearl reflects on Dimmesdale's two-faced behaviour towards her mother and herself, Hester scolds, 'Be quiet, Pearl! Thou understandest not these things' (p.200). What does Pearl not understand? Is the real problem that Pearl understands too clearly aspects of Dimmesdale's nature that Hester would like to ignore?

Chapters 23 and 24: 'The Revelation of the Scarlet Letter' and 'Conclusion' (pp.215–228)

Summary: Dimmesdale's death draws the story to a close.

Dimmesdale's sermon is received as inspired directly by God, but afterwards his brief spell of health and energy dissipates. He can barely walk out of the church. He gets as far as the scaffold of the pillory and, there, he sees Hester and Pearl. Pearl runs to embrace him and he asks Hester to help him up the scaffold steps. At the top, he addresses the crowd and confesses that he should have stood there seven years ago with Hester. He tears away his shirt:

> 'It was revealed! But it were irreverent to describe that revelation. For an instant the gaze of the horror-stricken multitude was concentrated on the ghastly miracle' (p.221).

We don't see what the multitude sees on Dimmesdale's naked chest, but it must be the same thing that Chillingworth saw there, which convinced him that Dimmesdale was Pearl's father. After baring his chest to the crowd, Dimmesdale sinks down to the platform. Hester whispers:

> 'Shall we not spend our immortal life together? Surely, surely, we have ransomed one another, with all this woe!' (p.222).

However, even with his dying breath, Dimmesdale is not ready to accept redemption.

After Dimmesdale's death, the people of Boston disagree about whether or not they had seen a scarlet A branded on Dimmesdale's chest. If they did see it, they disagree about how it came to be there. Once Dimmesdale is gone, Chillingworth no longer has revenge to live for and so he dies, leaving Pearl a large fortune. Pearl and Hester disappear for many years, but eventually Hester returns to Boston. The letters and gifts she exchanges with someone abroad make people think Pearl must be alive and happy somewhere, but missing her mother. Hester still wears her scarlet letter and is sorry for her sin, but the community no longer treats her as an outcast. Women frequently seek her advice and she dreams of a day when men and women will meet 'on a surer ground of mutual happiness' (p.227).

Q Hawthorne writes that the moral of Dimmesdale's story is, 'Be true! Show freely to the world, if not your worst, yet some trait whereby the worst may be inferred!' (p.224). What does Hawthorne mean by this? Do you agree with this advice?

CHARACTERS & RELATIONSHIPS

Hester Prynne

Key quotes

'Wondrous strength and generosity of a woman's heart! She will not speak!'
(p.63)

'Here, she said to herself, had been the scene of her guilt, and here should
be the scene of her earthly punishment; and so, perchance, the torture of her
daily shame would at length purge her soul, and work out another purity than
that which she had lost; more saint-like, because the result of martyrdom.'
(p.73)

'Hester comforted and counselled them, as best she might. She assured them,
too, of her firm belief, that, at some brighter period, when the world should
have grown ripe for it, in Heaven's own time, a new truth would be revealed,
in order to establish the whole relation between man and woman on a surer
ground of mutual happiness.' (p.227)

Hester Prynne, a tall, beautiful, young brunette from England, marries
a much older man. She is then sent to Boston ahead of him and lives
there for two years without even knowing whether he is alive or dead.
Considering her loneliness and the passion, independence and sensuality
of her spirit, it is hardly any wonder that she should fall in love with a
brilliant young minister there.

However, Hester's independence should neither be confused with
selfishness nor her passion and sensuality for hedonism (devotion to
pleasure-seeking). Even though she loves Arthur Dimmesdale and Pearl,
she is genuinely sorry for having betrayed Roger Chillingworth and her
holy marriage vows. She spends much of the book either seeking out
those in trouble so that she can help them, even if they despise her
(p.140), or meditating on right and wrong, sin and redemption (pp.143–
45). She channels her sensuality into the creation of gorgeous works of
textile art, both for sale and to express her love for her child.

Even her stubborn refusal to reveal the identity of her lover to the magistrates comes from a sense of honour and feelings of responsibility for him. Hester is willing and eager to bear his pain and punishment for him. When she comes to realise that simply having his secret kept has not been enough to protect his spirit from grief and trouble, she proposes leaving Boston and makes all the necessary practical arrangements. All along, of course, she takes the labour and expense of raising their daughter entirely upon herself.

Thus, though branded a sinner and a scarlet woman, Hester Prynne embodies the principle of responsibility far more fully than any other character in the novel. She never blames any other character for her sins and does not correct them when they blame her for theirs. She seeks no gain from other people and gives generously to anyone who needs it. She devotes herself steadfastly to the education and salvation of her daughter, and to the service of a community that rejects her. Hester's dedication and sense of responsibility marks Hawthorne's brand of individualism as special: she is tempted to run away from her community, but she is ultimately neither a hermit nor an isolationist. Hester thinks for herself, develops values at odds with those of her community, and carves out a living for herself when none seem possible, and yet she vigorously pursues the greater good before her own interests.

Pearl

Key quotes

'See ye not, she is the scarlet letter, only capable of being loved, and so endowed with a million-fold the power of retribution for my sin?' (p.100)

'In the little chaos of Pearl's character, there might be seen emerging – and could have been, from the very first – the stedfast [sic] principles an unflinching courage, – an uncontrollable will, – a sturdy pride, which might be disciplined into self-respect, – and a bitter scorn of many things which, when examined, might be found to have the taint of falsehood in them.' (p.157)

'A spell was broken. The great scene of grief, in which the wild infant bore a part, had developed all her sympathies; and as her tears fell upon her father's cheek, they were the pledge that she would grow up amid human joy and sorrow, nor for ever do battle with the world, but be a woman in it.' (p.222)

Over the course of the novel, Hester Prynne and Arthur Dimmesdale's illegitimate child, Pearl, grows from infancy to seven years of age (in 1649, the year of Governor John Winthrop's death and, later, Arthur Dimmesdale's) and, in the final chapter, into adulthood.

As an infant, Pearl is simply the physical representation of her mother's sin. As she grows into a little girl, Hester maintains Pearl's connection to her sin by dressing her in elaborately embroidered scarlet clothes that visually echo the elaborately embroidered badge on her bosom. Pearl retains the inhuman quality of a symbol. The text frequently refers to her as elfin, fairylike – a creature from the spirit world. She is capricious and unsympathetic to people (especially Arthur Dimmesdale, who repeatedly sets off her innate detector of falsehood), but she does seem to have a special link with nature: animals and even flowers seem to love her. Boston's Puritans whisper that she is the child of Satan. It is likely that this rumour has more to do with Hester's status as an outcast than with anything about Pearl herself, although Pearl is more lively and playful than the other Puritan children.

Pearl's link with nature, her intuitive sense of truth and falsehood, and even her elfin quality, are all in keeping with Romantic ideas about childhood. According to European and American Romantics, children are born good – they are natural and nature is good – and only become corrupted as they are inducted into human society. Romantic children are innocent, perceptive, asexual, ahistorical and timeless. They have a special access to truth, God and the spirit world that corrupt adults cannot achieve. This Romantic view of children and childhood replaced older ideas of children as small adults, born with original sin and, therefore, in need of correction if they are to achieve salvation. Much of the Romantic view persists in our culture to this day, despite the fact that later thinkers have challenged it (psychoanalytic critics, for example, have suggested that children are selfish and pleasure-seeking until they are taught to consider the needs of others).

Despite her change at the end of the novel, perhaps even because of it, Pearl remains a symbol and marker of her parents' spiritual status. When she becomes warmer and more sympathetic, it is because her father has finally confessed his sin; when she grows up to be a happy wife and mother, and a grateful, loving daughter, she marks Hester as fully redeemed.

Arthur Dimmesdale

Key quotes

'The minister well knew – subtle, but remorseful hypocrite that he was! – the light in which his vague confession would be viewed … He had spoken the very truth, and transformed it into the veriest falsehood. And yet, by the constitution of his nature, he loved the truth, and loathed the lie, as few men ever did. Therefore, above all things else, he loathed his miserable self!' (p.126)

'Hither, likewise, would come … the young virgins who so idolized their minister, and had made a shrine for him in their white bosoms; which, now, by the way, in their hurry and confusion, they would scantly have given themselves time to cover with their kerchiefs.' (p.133)

'Alas, what a ruin has befallen thee! … Wilt thou die for very weakness? There is no other cause!' (p.171)

Arthur Dimmesdale is handsome, young, intelligent and successful. Everyone in Boston – from Governor Bellingham and Reverend John Wilson down to the recently converted young virgins – loves and respects him, and he craves their approval. 'Lost as my own soul is,' he says to explain his reluctance to confess his sin or flee with Hester, 'I would still do what I may for other human souls! I dare not quit my post' (p.172). However, he is closer to honest about his reasons when he is speaking publicly of himself in the third person:

> 'Take heed how thou deniest to him – who, perchance, hath not the courage to grasp it for himself – the bitter, but wholesome, cup of punishment and repentance' (p.62).

Dimmesdale doesn't have the courage to share responsibility for his affair with Hester (or to share responsibility for raising their child) and he is even willing to let Hester take responsibility for his cowardly silence.

Dimmesdale's penances take secret, yet always dramatic and even stagey, forms: he whips himself; and he may or may not have a scarlet letter matching Hester's branded into the flesh of his chest, and that brand may or may not be self-inflicted. He also has Hester and Pearl rehearse with him, at night and in the forest, the confession and repentance he is unwilling to perform in public until he is just about to die. Dimmesdale fantasises about that confession, focusing not on the change in his own heart, or on God's or Hester and Pearl's response, but on the reaction of his adoring congregation – especially those young virgins who 'grew pale around him, victims of a passion so imbued with religious sentiment that they imagined it to be all religion, and brought it openly, in their white bosoms, as their most acceptable sacrifice before the altar' (p.125).

Still, Arthur Dimmesdale is not malicious. He admires Hester's strength and candour, and he would like to be the saint that the people of Boston think he is. He is simply weak – hollow at the core – and never grasps, as Hester does, that it is through accepting painful experiences and responsibility that one becomes strong enough to bear those burdens.

Roger Chillingworth

Key quotes

'In a word, old Roger Chillingworth was a striking evidence of man's faculty of transforming himself into a devil, if he will only, for a reasonable space of time, undertake a devil's office.' (p.148)

When Hester Prynne marries the man we know as Roger Chillingworth, he is a mild and benign scholar of alchemy – somewhat withdrawn from people and, perhaps, a bit selfish for marrying a beautiful young woman when he is an old man, but well-meaning, motivated chiefly by the desire for knowledge.

In the Romantic view, however, a scientific desire for knowledge can easily turn into the sin of hubris – insolence stemming from excessive pride, taking on offices that belong to God. This theme is most famously explored in Mary Shelley's *Frankenstein* (1818), but Hawthorne himself also examined it in the stories 'The Birthmark' (1843) and 'Rappaccini's Daughter' (1844). Hester reminds Chillingworth that vengeance belongs to God but, somewhat like Dimmesdale, Chillingworth is unwilling to take responsibility for his response to Dimmesdale's sin (though he is able to admit he was wrong to marry Hester and is, therefore, able to forgive her).

'It is not granted me to pardon. I have no such power' (p.152).

He pursues his revenge at the expense of not only his immortal soul, but also his physical life: once Dimmesdale has died, Chillingworth's obsession collapses and he has nothing left to live for. He does, however, perform one act of kindness in death: he leaves Pearl a large fortune.

Governor Bellingham

Key quotes

'He was not ill fitted to be the head and representative of a community, which owed its origin and progress ... [to] the somber sagacity of age; accomplishing so much, precisely because it imagined and hoped so little.' (p.59)

The real Richard Bellingham served as governor of Massachusetts from 1641 until his death in 1672. Hawthorne's character is stern and highly respected. In the novel he represents Puritan Boston's ruling class and hierarchy of legal power in general. He and the other magistrates are slower to forgive Hester Prynne than the ordinary people of Boston. In fact, he wants to take Pearl away from Hester, but Dimmesdale helps Hester to talk him out of it.

Governor Bellingham is wealthy. Hawthorne points out that men of his class have a much more luxurious lifestyle than most of Boston's Puritans. The implication is that Hawthorne sees the Puritan leaders as hypocrites who deny and punish others' pleasures while enjoying their own.

Mistress Hibbins

'Hester Prynne [felt] Mistress Hibbins to be of infirm mind; yet [Hester was] strangely startled and awe-stricken by the confidence with which she affirmed a personal connection between so many persons (herself among them) and the Evil One.' (pp.209–210)

The real Ann Hibbins may or may not have been the real Richard Bellingham's sister. She was hanged for witchcraft in Boston in 1656. Hawthorne's character is definitely Governor Bellingham's sister. She lives in the Governor's house and wears sumptuous clothes. Mistress Hibbins may be insane. She openly talks about meeting with Satan but, within *The Scarlet Letter*, she faces no legal punishments and suffers only a bad reputation. This may indicate how wealth and powerful connections can protect a person. Her status as Governor Bellingham's sister also shows how closely unabashed evil, in Hawthorne's world, can live with respectable authority.

Reverend John Wilson

'John Wilson, the eldest clergyman of Boston, [was] a great scholar ... and withal a man of kind and genial spirit. This last attribute, however, had been less carefully developed than his intellectual gifts, and was, in truth, rather a matter of shame than self-congratulation with him.' (p.60)

The real John Wilson taught at First Church in Boston from 1630 until his death in 1667. Hawthorne's character is Arthur Dimmesdale's spiritual and professional mentor, and a close friend of Governor Bellingham, with whom he shared a similar taste for luxury. Reverend Wilson 'was a grandfatherly sort of personage, and usually a vast favorite with children' (p.98), but not with Pearl.

The Puritans of Boston

'A throng of bearded men, in sad-colored garments and gray, steeple-crowned hats, intermixed with women, some wearing hoods, and others bareheaded, was assembled in front of a wooden edifice ...' (p.45)

'Amongst any other population, or at a later period in the history of New England, the grim rigidity that petrified the bearded physiognomies of these good people would have augured some awful business in hand.' (p.47)

Boston's Puritans comprise a composite character in *The Scarlet Letter* that, like a Greek chorus, indicate prevailing attitudes and normative (mainstream, authorised) values. The Puritans are dour, judgemental, and always gossiping, but they can also forgive or be kind. Their changing views of Hester Prynne – from scorn and disgust at the novel's beginning, to love and respect at its end – reflect her changing views of herself and, possibly, the progress of her relationship with God as she works to make up for her sin.

THEMES, IDEAS & VALUES

Outward and visible signs, inward and spiritual states

Which matters more: what you are inside or what you do, essences or actions? What is the relationship between spiritual truths and physical manifestations? Hawthorne's exploration of these topics is what makes *The Scarlet Letter* feel like psychological fiction even though, in 1850, psychology had not even been invented.

Since the sixteenth century (i.e. the century before the events of *The Scarlet Letter*), the Church of England has defined a sacrament, such as marriage, ordination, baptism or the Eucharist, as 'an outward and visible sign of an inward and spiritual grace' (*Book of Common Prayer* 1979, p.857). In conferring sacraments, the clergy ritualistically perform such outward and visible signs to both produce and celebrate such inward experiences of blessing in their parishioners.

In *The Scarlet Letter*, we don't see many blessings being conferred; rather, the ritualistic role of the clergy seems to be to punish. The punishment Hester Prynne suffers is a kind of inverted sacrament: she must wear the letter as an outward, physical mark of her inward, spiritual corruption. The Puritan leaders know of Hester's sin only because her body has visibly betrayed her: she has become pregnant and borne a child.

Arthur Dimmesdale, whose body keeps the secret that he is Hester's partner in crime, dies a slow spiritual and physical death over the course of the book because he is unable to confess and claim his mark of shame. By the novel's end though, his body may or may not bear its own mark – a mark that may or may not have been produced spontaneously. Other characters, too, bear the marks of their spiritual states: little Pearl, the child born in sin, is dressed to mirror her mother's badge of shame; and Roger Chillingworth, obsessed with revenge, spontaneously ages, his skin darkening and his eyes glowing in response to his new fiendlike pursuit.

Just as bodies can reveal inward states, the weather can reveal characters' spiritual secrets. When Hester and Dimmesdale joyfully agree to leave Boston, the forest fills with sunshine; when they stand at night on the scaffold, the sky lights up with an A-shaped, scarlet comet.

Outward appearances and actions are tricky to interpret and can be misleading, particularly in characters who have something to hide. Such tension between appearance and inner life creates much of the interest we feel in both Hester Prynne – who displays dutiful servitude and whose beauty appears dulled even when she is at her most free intellectually – and Arthur Dimmesdale – whose congregation sees him as a saint while he knows he is guilty not only of fornication, but also of hypocrisy.

Their rich, struggling, inner lives make these characters interesting and sympathetic to readers, but it is their outer actions – will Hester continue to wear the scarlet letter, will Dimmesdale finally confess? – that seem to determine whether they will find redemption. Thus, Hawthorne manages to leave open the question of which is more important, action or essence – if they can be separated at all.

Gender roles

Hester Prynne's exclusion from Puritan society results from her failure to properly perform her role as a woman: to be a faithful wife. It could also be the result of her being *too* essentially feminine: she falls in passionate, lifelong love with a man other than her husband. Hester is a failure as a wife (though neither Chillingworth nor Dimmesdale prove especially dependable to her, either), but she is a fiercely devoted mother, a tender helper to those in need and a reliable keeper of Dimmesdale's secret. She even makes her living through the feminine art of embroidery. The Puritans admire her needlework, even as they disapprove of some of the uses to which she puts her skill, such as Pearl's whimsical dresses, Hester's rich gown on the day of her public shaming and the fantastic flourishes of the scarlet letter itself.

If Hester is clearly the wrong kind of woman for the Puritans, she seems to be the right kind for Hawthorne – at least some of the time. He describes her as 'lady-like ... after the manner of the feminine gentility of those days; characterized by a certain state and dignity' (p.50). In ministering to the suffering, 'Hester's nature showed itself warm and rich;

a well-spring of human tenderness' (p.141); she brings to their care 'a woman's strength' (p.141) and she occupies her thoughts with questions that have 'reference to the whole race of womanhood' (p.144). However, as the solitary circumstances of her life turn her attention 'from passion and feeling, to thought' (p.143), Hawthorne reports:

> 'Some attribute had departed from her, the permanence of which had been essential to keep her a woman' (p.143).

Although Hawthorne seems to mourn Hester's loss of femininity and physical beauty, he confers upon her androgyny a cross-gendered power to act. Just after Hester's 'attribute ... depart[s]' (p.143), we learn that she has 'resolved to ... do what might be in her power for the rescue of the victim' (p.146) of her former husband's revenge. In setting herself this mission to rescue Dimmesdale, Hester casts herself as the powerful romantic hero, with Dimmesdale obligingly playing the passive damsel in distress, begging, 'Think for me, Hester! Thou art strong. Resolve for me!' (p.171).

The joy that Hester takes in being strong for Dimmesdale allows her to briefly regain her feminine beauty, as if beauty were a reward for progress on her manly quest. Is Hawthorne celebrating her androgyny? Is she a Joan of Arc figure, romantic and admirable for her very gender transgression? Ultimately, her quest to save Dimmesdale fails and he dies. However, his death results not from any lack of feminine tenderness or chivalrous courage on Hester's part, but from his own lack of masculine resolve. For Hawthorne, it seems characters who aspire to goodness, yet know themselves to be flawed and human, can survive only if they man up – and that goes for women, too.

Romantic passion: a trap?

As Nina Baym points out in *The Scarlet Letter: A Reading* (1986), the romance plot in Hawthorne's novel – our sympathetic desire for Hester to get her man – is at odds with Hester's more important goal: to be accepted by the Puritan community not as a hypocritical plaster saint like Dimmesdale, but as herself, as she really is – imperfect, feeling, striving, human. If Hester and Dimmesdale had succeeded in their plan to escape Boston together, both would have been forever stained in the community's opinion. They would have gone forth as an isolated couple (or family, with Pearl), alone against the world, and this would have been a very different novel.

However, would this have meant a 'happy ending' for Hester? Dimmesdale is entirely self-involved. He looks to Hester for tenderness and strength, but never asks himself what he can offer her in return. For the first seven years of Pearl's life, Dimmesdale chose his career and having the community's approval over the opportunity to support, raise and love her. Even when he finally acknowledges Pearl and Hester at the novel's end, Dimmesdale does so only to dramatise his own sin, torment and confession, not to offer them any comfort or fidelity. Assessed in this light, Dimmesdale does not make a very attractive romantic prospect.

In fact, the kindest thing any man does for Hester Prynne in *The Scarlet Letter* occurs when Roger Chillingworth unofficially dissolves their marriage. Dimmesdale brings her nothing but shame and disappointment, despite her unwavering devotion to him. Baym writes that 'romantic love serves Hester so badly' that Hawthorne seems to present 'the idea of romantic love as a trick to ensure the willing subservience of women to the social system' (Baym 1986, p.xxix).

As it stands, Dimmesdale's death deprives Hester (and us) of her love story's happy ending, but it allows her to win a larger social victory: at the novel's end, she is a beloved advisor to the women of Boston. That a convicted adulteress could gain such social redemption and acceptance indicates that Boston has become, as Hester had hoped, a kinder and more tolerant society. As Baym writes, 'Hester has ... changed the Puritans more than they have changed her' (Baym 1986, p.29).

Free will vs. fate

A fundamental difference between the Romantic understanding of the world and that of Hawthorne's Puritan ancestors has to do with the question of who controls human actions. Puritans believed that God had foreordained every event in the history of the universe, including which souls would go to heaven and which ones would not. The Romantics' belief in humanism suggested that people were in charge of their own actions and destinies, a viewpoint that also has a long Christian tradition (though Romantic-era love stories do often indicate the influence of fate). *The Scarlet Letter* is full of signs of Hawthorne's wrestling with the question of free will versus predestination (fate).

Early in the novel, Hawthorne's ascription of apparently unchanging essences to his characters makes them seem powerless to change their fates. Hester Prynne, we are told, has 'an impulsive and passionate nature' (p.53) that seems to explain her crime. Arthur Dimmesdale's mouth, which 'unless when he forcibly compressed it, was apt to be tremulous, expressing both nervous sensibility and a vast power of self-restraint' (p.61), seems to carry, encoded within its flesh, his inevitable inner turmoil. Pearl seems fated to a tragic and criminal end from her very conception:

> 'In giving her existence, a great law had been broken; and the result was a being, whose elements were perhaps beautiful and brilliant, but all in disorder' (p.81).

However, as the novel progresses we see signs that neither Hester nor Pearl is likely to submit to any fate except one that they choose. Hawthorne doesn't actually use the word 'wilful' to describe young Pearl, but he refers frequently to her 'caprices' and reports that despite her best efforts at discipline, 'Hester was ultimately compelled to stand aside, and permit the child to be swayed by her own impulses' (p.82). Hester has learned that she must choose her battles, but when it comes to something she really cares about, such as Pearl, she is willing to fight for her way.

> 'Alone in the world, cast off by it, and with this sole treasure to keep her heart alive, she felt that she possessed indefeasible rights against the world, and was ready to defend them to the death' (p.100).

Where another person might ascribe adversity to God's will, Hester is characterised by her confidence that there's always something she can do about it.

Moreover, in Chapter 8, 'The Elf-Child and the Minister,' the Puritan clergy seems to believe in free will (Nina Baym points this out in *The Scarlet Letter: A Reading* 1986, pp.35–6, to support her argument that Hawthorne's Bostonians behave more like Victorians than like historically accurate seventeenth-century Puritans). In his argument for Hester being allowed to keep and raise Pearl, Dimmesdale describes Pearl as 'an infant immortality, a being capable of eternal joy or sorrow, confided to [Hester's] care ... if she bring the child to heaven, the child also will bring its parent thither!' (pp.101–2). Dimmesdale clearly imagines that the fates of Pearl and Hester's eternal souls are not predestined, but dependent upon Hester's actions. Since this argument easily wins Governor Bellingham and Reverend John Wilson over, it would appear that they are not especially invested in the idea of predestination either.

Free will is not a settled fact in the novel, though. As the story builds towards its final act, we see Hester arguing in favour of free will in conversations with Chillingworth and Dimmesdale, both of whom take fatalist (believing that how events happen cannot be changed and cannot be avoided) stances in order to avoid responsibility for their own actions. To Chillingworth, Hester says, 'thou hast been deeply wronged, and hast it at thy will to pardon' (p.152); to Dimmesdale, 'Heaven would show mercy ... hadst thou but the strength to take advantage of it' (p.171) and 'Thou art free! ... Hast thou exhausted possibility in the failure of this one trial? Not so! The future is yet full of trial and success' (p.172). She tells him that torments 'have made thee feeble to will and to do! – [and] will leave thee powerless even to repent!' (p.173). These remarks make it clear that, for Hester, free will and human responsibility are essential parts of a person's relationship with God. She urges each man to choose actions that will reconcile him with divine will. The men sound eerily alike as they demur: 'The judgment of God is on me ... it is too mighty for me to struggle with!' (p.171), insists Dimmesdale; Chillingworth says, 'I have no such power ... it has all been a dark necessity ... It is our fate' (p.152).

The fate or destiny created by the author in his narrative arc is one reason why some critics have read Hawthorne as not entirely sympathetic to Hester's thoughts and actions. Though Hester is an attractive character, Hawthorne (or God, or fate) does seem to punish her by frustrating her desire for a fully realised relationship with Dimmesdale and by having her live out her life alone in a cottage on the edge of Boston, the scarlet letter on her breast. However, we can also view a reconciliation between divine justice and human free will as Hester's final spiritual triumph. For Hester, true repentance and true obedience to God are the products of a will that chooses God freely. At the end of the novel, Hester chooses to submit to her destiny:

> 'She had returned, therefore, and resumed, – of her own free will ...
> the symbol of which we have related so dark a tale' (p.227).

The artist and society

From reading 'The Custom-House,' we know that Hawthorne was anxious about the consequences of his artistic inclinations both for his finances – he seems to always be choosing between writing stories or making money – and his worth in the eyes of his family and community, represented by the imaginary Puritan ancestors who dismiss him as an 'idler', a 'degenerate' and mere 'writer of storybooks' who 'might as well have been a fiddler' (p.13). 'The Custom-House' aligns Hawthorne with Hester in his gesture of placing the scarlet letter over his own heart (p.32). In the main text, Hester resembles Hawthorne in that she is the novel's only character who uses creativity both professionally and for personal expression. Her beautiful, imaginative needlework can be seen in christening gowns and ministers' vestments (to earn money), and in the scarlet letter itself, her gown for her day of punishment and Pearl's clothes (for personal expression).

If Hester is Hawthorne's representative in the novel, then perhaps he has used her to explore questions about the role of the artist in society. Is an artist a rebel, outcast and criminal or a necessary and beloved community member? Is it possible for an artist to be a good parent and provide for his/her family? Is art hedonistic (selfishly pleasure-seeking) or socially responsible? Is artistic skill an inborn essence or an outward, chosen and disciplined action? As Hawthorne answers these questions about Hester in *The Scarlet Letter*, we can imagine him answering them about himself, too.

DIFFERENT INTERPRETATIONS

Different interpretations arise from different responses to a text. Over time, a text will give rise to a wide range of responses from its readers, who may come from various social or cultural groups and live in very different places and historical periods. These responses can be published in newspapers, journals and books by critics and reviewers or they can be expressed in discussions among readers in the media, classrooms, book clubs and so on. While there is no single correct reading or interpretation of a text, it is important to understand that an interpretation is more than a personal opinion; it is the justification of a point of view on the text. To present an interpretation of the text based on your point of view you must use a logical argument and support it with relevant evidence from the text.

Critical viewpoints

The Scarlet Letter has never gone out of print since it was first published and it has received a great deal of critical attention right from the start. In 1879, Henry James declared it not only Hawthorne's best work, but:

> '... the finest piece of imaginative writing yet put forth in the United States – a kind of literary declaration of independence which founds the American novel tradition as distinct from its British ancestors and cousins' (Scharnhorst 1992, p.xviii).

However, its initial critical reception in the US was not all positive. Whereas British critics immediately praised its emotional perceptiveness, many American critics in the 1850s found it immoral either because of its mockery of Hawthorne's former colleagues in 'The Custom-House', the main story's criticism of religious leaders, or the raciness of the subject matter – the dirty story of 'a fornicator, an adulteress and their illegitimate child' (Scharnhorst 1992, p.xv).

Over the years, *The Scarlet Letter* has maintained a central place in the American literary canon (list of books regarded as 'high' literature and frequently taught in high schools and universities), although the aspects of the book that have made it important to people have changed many times over the years. As Jane Tompkins writes in *Sensational Designs: The Cultural Work of American Fiction 1790–1860*, 'The Scarlet Letter is a great novel in 1850, in 1876, in 1904, in 1942, and in 1966, but each time it is great for different reasons' (1986, p.35).

For example, in the mid-twentieth century, most critics were interested in *The Scarlet Letter* either from a formalist perspective (analysing its carefully symmetrical plot arc and its complex, sophisticated sentence structure) or from a psychoanalytic perspective (delving into the internal psychological motivations and conflicts of Hester Prynne and especially of Arthur Dimmesdale). Over the past fifty years, these two sets of concerns have largely given way to three others. New Historicist critics have been interested in what the novel tells us about Nathaniel Hawthorne's political and literary context, and especially how Americans of the 1840s used their understanding and interpretation of Americans of the 1640s to comment upon or better understand their own historical period. Feminist critics have pointed to Hester as the first great American literary heroine and have asked questions about how Hawthorne represents masculinity and femininity, sexuality, motherhood and the power relations between men and women. Post-structuralist critics have paid attention to the many ambiguities and open-ended questions in the text; they have mapped the power structures encoded both in Hawthorne's writing and in the reading practices we bring to it, and they have noted how readers are invited to interpret the novel and thus to participate in creating its meaning.

Three contrasting interpretations

Literary texts abound with multiple, often contradictory meanings. This is part of what keeps them exciting generation after generation and part of what makes us want to reread them at different moments in our own lives. How you interpret a text depends on your priorities, your focus and your world view. You can think of the result as a collaboration, a conversation or even an argument between you and the text's author.

Interpretation 1: *The Scarlet Letter* is the story of Hester Prynne's struggle against harsh, repressive Puritan society

The Scarlet Letter begins and ends with Hester Prynne. Of all the characters in the novel, she appears the most and the letter for which the novel is named adorns the bosom of her dress. She is clearly the main character. Moreover, Hawthorne sets readers up to like her and take her side. When we first meet her, we learn that she is young, beautiful, elegant and ladylike, yet there is 'something exquisitely painful' (p.50) in her beauty. Meanwhile, her antagonists – the Puritans who view her with scorn – are 'grim' and their sympathy is 'Meagre, indeed, and cold' (p.47). Hawthorne carefully associates them with their 'gloomy', 'ponderous' and 'ugly' prison, the 'black flower of civilized society' (p.47), while linking Hester with 'a wild rose-bush, covered, in this month of June, with its delicate gems' (p.45) that may 'symbolize some sweet moral blossom' (p.46). Thus, he lets us know that Hester is not only beautiful, but also both morally good and wild. The Puritans who are punishing her are not ugly, but also repressive and civilised.

Over the course of the novel, Puritan society attacks the heroine again and again. First, she is made to stand for three hours on the scaffold and be grilled about her lover. Next, she is made to wear the scarlet letter for the rest of her life – some members of the crowd even suggest that it should be burned into her flesh or that she be executed! Three years later, even though she has committed no new crime, the leaders of the town contemplate punishing her further by removing her child from her custody. All along, the watchful gaze of the Puritan town has prevented Hester from spending any time alone with Arthur Dimmesdale, the man she loves. Near the end of the novel, she realises that Puritan values – along with her jealous former husband – are persecuting her beloved and pushing him into an early grave. Finally, she watches him die in her arms. The Puritans could hardly do more to make Hester's life miserable.

Hester's response, though, is mild, inviting us to love her even more. She 'bestowed all her superfluous means in charity' (p.75); 'she was patient, – a martyr, indeed' (p.77); and she confesses to her husband, 'I have greatly wronged thee' (p.68). However, she is not entirely submissive. When Governor Bellingham wants to take away her child, Hester 'felt that she possessed indefeasible rights against the world, and was ready to defend them to the death' (p.100). As time goes on, the Puritans' antipathy (enmity, dislike) towards Hester lessens and 'a species of general regard had ultimately grown up in reference to Hester Prynne' (p.140). Hester, on the other hand, though still 'self-ordained a Sister of Mercy' (p.141), becomes much more rebellious in her thoughts:

> 'The world's law was no law for her mind … She assumed a freedom of speculation … which our forefathers, had they known of it, would have held to be a deadlier crime than her adultery' (p.143).

Reversing her original shame and penitence for the latter act, she eventually says to her lover, 'What we did had a consecration of its own' (p.170). Hester has become a true rebel and outlaw.

It is not clear who prevails in this story – Hester or the Puritans. On the one hand, Hester's lover dies young and she grows old alone on the outskirts of Boston, still wearing her badge of shame. These facts make the ending seem like a sad one for Hester, as if she is being justly punished for her sins. On the other hand, her lover's death may be a blessing in disguise, since he is not a very generous or helpful partner. Besides, in losing him, she gains the lifelong love and support of her previously fairly unsympathetic child. Furthermore, Hester chooses to spend year after year serving her penance; this is not a fate that is forced upon her. Finally, in her later years, the Puritans no longer scorn but instead respect Hester. Perhaps she has triumphed after all.

Interpretation 2: *The Scarlet Letter* is the story of Arthur Dimmesdale's struggle with himself

Although Hester Prynne appears in the story before him and departs after he does, Arthur Dimmesdale is the main character of *The Scarlet Letter*. His inner struggle is the focus of the book and it makes him the most unpredictable and, therefore, the most interesting character. Besides, everyone in the book, with the possible exception of the hard-hearted little Pearl, is in love with him. *The Scarlet Letter* is the tragedy of a man felled by his three conflicting desires: for God's love, for the community's love and for a woman's love.

Within the deeply religious world of *The Scarlet Letter*, God's love is more or less synonymous with self-respect. Every character, to a greater or lesser degree, wants God's love. Dimmesdale himself says that without his faith, he would be 'a man devoid of conscience, – a wretch with coarse and brutal instincts' (p.166), and no one wants to be a wretch. The sense that he has fallen from God's grace makes Dimmesdale feel like 'an accursed thing' (p.125) and, because he is a sensitive man with a 'strange sympathy betwixt soul and body' (p.120), it also makes him physically ill. However, as much as Dimmesdale wants to respect himself by being in accord with God, his desire for Hester causes him to sin and his desire for the community's love prevents him from confessing and seeking forgiveness.

Of Dimmesdale's three desires, the community's love seems to be the one he is most successful in securing. (Could this be because it is the one he wants most?) We learn early on that some members of the community 'declared, that, if Mr Dimmesdale were ... going to die, it was cause enough, that the world was not worth to be any longer trodden by his feet' (p.106). In fact, Dimmesdale's reputation only improves as the story continues. His three harshest critics are himself, Chillingworth and little Pearl. If his constant fantasies about a dramatic confession and his overwhelming concern for his own comfort and reputation are any indication, Dimmesdale loves himself dearly even if he can't respect himself. Chillingworth is so obsessed with revenging Dimmesdale's crime that he dies once he is deprived of Dimmesdale. Hawthorne writes:

> 'It is a curious subject of observation and inquiry, whether hatred and love be not the same thing ... the two passions seem essentially the same' (p.225).

As we see at the end of Chapter 10, 'The Leech and His Patient', Chillingworth takes the first possible opportunity to peek inside Dimmesdale's clothes at his naked chest, a sight that fills Chillingworth with 'ecstasy' (p.121). Even Pearl, who sometimes refuses Dimmesdale's affection, offers him early in the book 'a caress so tender' (p.102) and also bathes the dying man's face in her tears. Her usual reserve with him seems mainly to result from his repeated denial of her requests to publicly acknowledge his relationship to her. To confess his paternity, though, would be to confess that he has given in to his desire for a woman – and this would lose him the community's esteem.

Dimmesdale's dilemma results from his desire for a woman's love – and it may not matter to him which woman's. Nowhere in the book does he seem to think of Hester as special or as an especially attractive woman, but since she knows his secret, he can let down his guard with her. His having slept with her seems in accord with his thoughts about his young female parishioners in general. As he stands on the scaffold at midnight, he fantasises:

> 'Hither, likewise, would come ... the young virgins who so idolized their minister, and had made a shrine for him in their white bosoms; which, now, by the by, in their hurry and confusion, they would scantly have given themselves time to cover with their kerchiefs' (p.133).

Returning home after his meeting in the woods with Hester, he encounters 'the youngest sister of them all ... fair and pure as a lily that had bloomed in Paradise. The minister knew well that he was himself enshrined within the stainless sanctity of her heart' (p.191). Dimmesdale has acted upon his desire only 'in a single instance' (p.174), but it is easy enough to imagine Hester's as just another fair, white bosom in which he would like to be enshrined.

Dimmesdale's desire to be loved by a woman is, in part, simply an extension of his desire to be loved by all. He wants a woman to love him so that she will take care of him. 'Be thou strong for me!' (p.171), Dimmesdale implores Hester. He is filled with joy, not at the thought of escaping Boston with this particular woman, but at the thought that he will not have to go alone. In this light, it's not so surprising that Dimmesdale lets Chillingworth move in with him, even though the old man gives Dimmesdale the creeps. Chillingworth is stronger than Dimmesdale; in his capacity as a physician, he takes care of Dimmesdale and hardly lets him be alone for a single moment. Dimmesdale, with his interest in 'white bosoms' (pp.125, 133), would probably prefer to be taken care of by a woman, but if it makes his adoring congregation happier, Chillingworth will do. Although Dimmesdale's desire for a woman's love is what got him into trouble, it comes into play very little – and then only quite passively – as the story unfolds.

Because we know Dimmesdale is motivated by three desires and that there is no way, in his present circumstances, for all three to be satisfied, he is the central character in *The Scarlet Letter*. The narrative hinges upon the question: which desire will win out? What will Dimmesdale do to resolve the conflict between his three desires? Can he ever be happy? Apparently he cannot. Even after his confession, as he dies in Hester's arms, Dimmesdale doesn't seem confident of his ultimate redemption. However, his pessimism at this moment may be motivated more by the belief that he has lost his community's esteem than by the fear that God is not satisfied with his confession. In any case, Dimmesdale's sensitive body is too fragile to withstand the conflicting demands of his desires; at the tragedy's climax, they tear him apart.

Interpretation 3: *The Scarlet Letter* is the story of the shifting meanings of the letter itself and, thus, of the difficulty of establishing authority through language

The Scarlet Letter's central mystery is the mystery of its central, and title, character. The original meaning of the word **character** was not 'a fictional person', but 'the graphic representation of a number or letter'. This is not the kind of character we see in films, but the kind that has a limit of 140 on Twitter – though both forms, of course, are basic elements of a novel. This novel's main character is the letter that Hester Prynne wears pinned to her bosom and, like any main character, this one changes and grows through the course of the novel, moving through the pages with a will of its own.

The Puritan magistrates sentence Hester to wearing the scarlet letter as a mark of her shameful crime: 'A' for adulteress. However, from the first time we see the letter, it is already working to undercut and undo that meaning:

> 'It was so artistically done, and with so much fertility and gorgeous luxuriance of fancy, that it had all the effect of a last and fitting decoration to the apparel which she wore' (p.50).

Is the scarlet letter, then, a mark of shame or an ornament? Is this character a lifeless graphic mark or an entity with a will of its own? Can it be both? How certain can we be of what any symbol means?

> 'It had the effect of a spell, taking her out of the ordinary relations with humanity, and inclosing her in a sphere by herself' (p.51).

The magistrates intend to isolate Hester as a sinner and criminal by making her wear the letter, but before the novel's end the letter's effect will shift, marking Hester as a beautiful woman, as one possibly in communication with the devil, as one dedicated to service and, finally, as one particularly valued for her wisdom and generosity.

We are told that the letter is merely a piece of velvet embroidered with gold thread, but at various times in the novel it seems able to conduct supernatural light and heat:

> 'It was whispered, by those who peered after her, that the scarlet letter threw a lurid gleam along the dark passage-way of the interior' (p.64).

> '... they averred, that the symbol was not mere scarlet cloth ... but was red-hot with infernal fire and could be seen glowing all alight ... in the night-time. And we must needs say, it seared Hester's bosom ... deeply' (p.79).

In these instances, the letter seems to get its light and heat from the fire of Boston gossip, but a more impartial source also testifies to these qualities: Hawthorne himself. In 'The Custom-House', when he places the letter on his breast, Hawthorne writes:

> 'It seemed to me, then, that I experienced a sensation not
> altogether physical, yet almost so, as of burning heat; and as if
> the letter were not of red cloth, but red-hot iron' (p.32).

Hester informs Chillingworth that the letter is beyond the power of human authorities:

> 'It lies not in the pleasure of the magistrates to take off this badge
> ... Were I worthy to be quit of it, it would fall away of its own
> nature, or be transformed into something that should speak a
> different purport' (p.147).

Little Pearl, who Hester claims 'is the scarlet letter, only capable of being loved' (p.100), is obsessed with her mother's letter, sometimes creating imitations of it for her own chest. She asks over and over again what the letter means and Hester is unable to answer her (pp.155–58, 160–62). The people of Boston are no less obsessed. Although they are convinced at the novel's beginning that Hester is a criminal and that the A is her brand of shame, her good works begin to unsettle that meaning.

> 'She was self-ordained a Sister of Mercy ... The letter was the
> symbol of her calling ... They said that it meant Able; so strong
> was Hester Prynne, with a woman's strength' (p.141).

Rumour still invests the letter with supernatural power, but that power no longer seems infernal: 'It imparted to the wearer a kind of sacredness, which enabled her to walk securely amid all peril' (p.142), protecting her from thieves and from the arrows of Native Americans. On the night of Governor John Winthrop's death, a scarlet letter, which the Bostonians 'interpret to stand for Angel' (p.138), appears in the sky. If Governor Winthrop's scarlet A marks him as an angel, then how are we to read Hester Prynne's?

The letter's shifting significance introduces a broader thread of uncertainty to the novel. Referring to its supernatural properties, Hawthorne writes, 'the reader may smile, but must not doubt my word' (p.32) and 'perhaps there was more truth in the rumour than our modern incredulity may be inclined to admit' (p.79). At these moments, he acknowledges that readers may simply not believe the details of his story. At other times, Hawthorne himself does not seem to believe what he is writing: 'but here the tale has surely lapsed into the improbable' (p.178). If the author himself is uncertain of the truth of his story, then who can verify it? Hawthorne implies that there may be no authority who can ultimately fix meanings or guarantee absolute truth.

QUESTIONS & ANSWERS

This section focuses on your own analytical writing on the text, and gives you strategies for producing high-quality responses in your coursework and exam essays.

Essay writing – an overview

An essay is a formal and serious piece of writing that presents your point of view on the text, usually in response to a given essay topic. Your 'point of view' in an essay is your interpretation of the meaning of the text's language, structure, characters, situations and events, supported by detailed analysis of textual evidence.

Analyse – don't summarise

In your essay it is important to avoid simply summarising what happens in a text:

- A **summary** is a description or paraphrase (retelling in different words) of the characters and events. For example: 'Macbeth has a horrifying vision of a dagger dripping with blood before he goes to murder King Duncan'.

- An **analysis** is an explanation of the real meaning or significance that lies 'beneath' the text's words (and images, for a film). For example: 'Macbeth's vision of a bloody dagger shows how deeply uneasy he is about the violent act he is contemplating – as well as his sense that supernatural forces are impelling him to act'.

A limited amount of summary is sometimes necessary to let your reader know which part of the text you wish to discuss. However, always keep this to a minimum and follow it immediately with your analysis (explanation) of what this part of the text is really telling us.

Plan your essay

Carefully plan your essay so that you have a clear idea of what you are going to say. The plan ensures that your ideas flow logically, that your argument remains consistent and that you stay on the topic. An essay plan should be a list of **brief dot points** – no more than half a page. It includes:

- your central argument or main contention – a concise statement (usually in a single sentence) of your overall response to the topic (see 'Analysing a sample topic' for guidelines on how to formulate a main contention)

- three or four dot points for each paragraph indicating the main idea and evidence/examples from the text – note that in your essay you will need to expand on these points and analyse the evidence.

Structure your essay

An essay is a complete, self-contained piece of writing. It has a clear beginning (the introduction), middle (several body paragraphs) and end (the last paragraph or conclusion). It must also have a central argument that runs throughout, linking each paragraph to form a coherent whole.

See examples of introductions and conclusions in the 'Analysing a sample topic' and 'Sample answer' sections.

The introduction establishes your overall response to the topic. It includes your main contention and outlines the main evidence you will refer to in the course of the essay. Write your introduction *after* you have done a plan and *before* you write the rest of the essay.

The body paragraphs argue your case – they present evidence from the text and explain how this evidence supports your argument. Each body paragraph needs:

- a strong **topic sentence** (usually the first sentence) that states the main point being made in the paragraph

- **evidence** from the text, including some brief quotations

- **analysis** of the textual evidence, explaining its significance, and an **explanation** of how it supports your argument

- **links back to the topic** in one or more statements, usually towards the end of the paragraph.

Connect the body paragraphs so that your discussion flows smoothly. Use some linking words and phrases, such as 'similarly' and 'on the other hand', though don't start every paragraph like this. Another strategy is to use a significant word from the last sentence of one paragraph in the first sentence of the next.

Use key terms from the topic – or similes for them – throughout, so the relevance of your discussion to the topic is always clear.

The conclusion ties everything together and finishes the essay. It includes strong statements that emphasise your central argument and provide a clear response to the topic.

Avoid simply restating the points made earlier in the essay – this will end on a very flat note and imply that you have run out of ideas and vocabulary. The conclusion is meant to be a logical extension of what you have written, not just a repetition or summary of it. Writing an effective conclusion can be a challenge. Try using these tips:

- Start by linking back to the final sentence of the second-last paragraph – this helps your writing to 'flow', rather than just leaping back to your main contention straight away.

- Use similes and expressions with equivalent meanings to vary your vocabulary. This allows you to reinforce your line of argument without being repetitive.

- When planning your essay, think of one or two broad statements or observations about the text's wider meaning. These should be related to the topic and your overall argument. Keep them for the conclusion, since they will give you something 'new' to say, but still follow logically from your discussion. The introduction will be focused on the topic, but the conclusion can present a wider view of the text.

Essay topics

1   Why does Hawthorne open with a framing device, but not return to it at the end of the book?

2   Why is Mistress Hibbins in this story? What function does she serve?

3   Dimmesdale says, 'Of penance I have had enough! Of penitence
    there has been none!' (p.167). What is the difference between
    penance and penitence? What might this distinction reveal about
    Dimmesdale's character or about Puritan society as Hawthorne
    imagines it?

4   Does Hawthorne seem to think that Hester and Dimmesdale's most
    important mistake is sinning against God or breaking human-created
    social rules? Do they suffer because they have sinned or because
    they feel guilty?

5   Does Hester really know the real Dimmesdale? Is Hester in love
    with Dimmesdale as he really is or only with Dimmesdale as she
    imagines him to be?

6   Why is Roger Chillingworth so quick to forgive Hester and yet so
    obsessed with punishing Dimmesdale? Are the reasons that he gives
    Hester the whole truth?

7   Would leaving Boston have been the right thing for Dimmesdale to
    do? Would it have been the right thing for Hester to do? Why or why
    not?

8   Would Hawthorne agree with Hester when she tells Dimmesdale
    that 'what we did had a consecration of its own' (p.170)?

9   What is the role of witchcraft, Satan and the Black Man in this
    novel?

10 What is the role of the forest in this novel and what is the role of the
    town?

11 What does Arthur Dimmesdale mean to Pearl? Since she has
    seldom shown him any affection, why does his death affect her so
    profoundly?

12 In *The Scarlet Letter*, Pearl lives with Hester, Mistress Hibbins lives
    with Governor Bellingham and Roger Chillingworth lives with Arthur
    Dimmesdale. What does Hawthorne reveal about these characters
    through the people they live with?

13 Who wears beautiful clothes in this novel? What do beautiful clothes
    represent?

Vocabulary for writing on *The Scarlet Letter*

Ambiguity: Uncertainty of meaning arising from the ability to interpret one event or statement in a number of ways.

Antinomianism: The belief that one is exempt from moral laws.

Atone: To do penance in order to pay for a sin.

Doubling: The literary practice of pairing characters in order to draw attention to shared and/or opposite qualities in them.

Egalitarianism: The belief that people are equal in value and should have equal opportunities.

Expiation: Atonement; payment for a sin.

Feminism: The political pursuit of equality between men and women; a critical viewpoint that pays careful attention to gender roles and expectations.

Frame narrative: A story whose main events are presented as a story-within-a-story.

Heterodox: Differing from authorised teachings; unorthodox.

Hierarchy: A social structure in which some people are considered to be 'above' others in a series of levels; power is concentrated at the top.

Hypocrisy: A pretence of having values or virtues one does not actually have.

Individualism: A social outlook that stresses independence, self-reliance and valuing each person's unique talents, desires, beliefs and goals.

Irony: An idea or situation opposite to what might have been expected. Irony can be used for sarcastic or humorous purposes, but it can also heighten the emotional impact of a tragedy.

Predestination: The belief that God has foreordained everything that will happen; the opposite of free will (see 'Themes, Ideas & Values', Free will vs. fate).

Analysing a sample topic

Who wears beautiful clothes in this novel? What do beautiful clothes represent?

Begin by reading the question really carefully. What is the topic? (It may help you to underline key words in the question.) Is there more than one element that must be considered? (If there are multiple elements, you'll need to consider all aspects and the relationship between them. In this case, exploring who has beautiful clothes will probably help you to decide what clothes represent in *The Scarlet Letter*.) What ideas do you already have about this topic and why do they matter to you?

Consider the evidence

A strong analysis will be grounded firmly in the evidence at hand – that is, it will use quotations from the text as its foundation. Gather a list of quotes that tell you what you know about the topic. For each quotation, note what is interesting about it, how it works or what special light it sheds on your topic. Analysis is a bit like a maths problem; your essay will need to show all of your logical steps. You could also think of analysis as a tour of your thoughts: be a good tour guide and get your readers all the way from point A (the quotation) to point Z (the insight that quotation gives you into your topic) without losing them somewhere in between.

Devise your contention

You cannot devise your contention without considering the evidence first. Think about what the quotations you have collected have in common and the ways in which they might contradict one another. When you look at all the quotations about beautiful clothes in *The Scarlet Letter*, what story do they tell? You may decide that there is more than one contention to be made. In that case, choose either the one you that believe in the most (which you may find easiest to prove) or the one that you find most surprising and interesting (which you and your readers may find the most exciting).

Sample introduction

Though set in austere, Puritan, seventeenth-century New England, *The Scarlet Letter* shows a surprising interest in beautiful and heavily ornamented clothing. Its very title refers to a badge of red velvet and gold thread made to adorn the bodice of Hester Prynne's gowns. Hester – by trade and by creative inclination – is a full-time creator of intricate needlework. The novel's obsession with clothing seems less surprising when we consider its sustained interest in the relationship between outer, physical signs and inner, spiritual status. In *The Scarlet Letter*, the two groups of people who wear beautiful, rich clothing most often are wealthy, high-status characters and supposedly wicked characters (though we learn that most people in the community wear gorgeous things on momentous occasions in their lives, for example, when they are christened, married and buried). The distribution of rich clothing in *The Scarlet Letter* suggests that while wealth and high status are inextricable from sin and evil, sin and evil, like joy and virtue, are inevitable aspects of every human life.

Body paragraph 1

Beautiful clothes are a mark of wealth and high status in the community.

- **Governor Bellingham:** When we first meet him, we know he is a wealthy man because 'He wore a dark feather in his hat, a border of embroidery on his cloak, and a black velvet tunic beneath' (p.59). Later, in his home, we see him in 'an elaborate ruff' (p.96) and Dimmesdale later imagines him coming out 'with his King James's ruff fastened askew' (p.133). In fact, he is the only man whose clothes get any attention in this book, though we do learn that 'Deep ruffs, painfully wrought bands, and gorgeously embroidered gloves, were all deemed necessary to the official state of men assuming the reins of power' (p.74).

- **Mistress Hibbins:** Governor Bellingham's sister, the novel's only woman of wealth and high status, wears elaborate, expensive clothes: 'She made a very grand appearance; having a high head-dress, a rich velvet, and a ruff' (p.193). On another occasion she is 'arrayed in great magnificence, with a triple ruff, a broidered stomacher, a gown of rich velvet, and a gold-headed cane' (p.209). Her clothes mark her as a 'gentlewoman', even if her behaviour is 'weird' (p.210).

- **Sumptuary laws:** These laws enforce the requirement for the average Puritan to wear drab, inexpensive clothing most of the time. The novel's opening sentence describes these ugly clothes: 'bearded men, in sad-colored garments and gray, steeple-crowned hats, intermixed with women, some wearing hoods' (p.45). Later, the novel refers to 'the sable simplicity that generally characterized the Puritanic modes of dress' (p.74). We learn that sumptuary laws forbade 'extravagances [of dress] to the plebeian order', but that Hester's skill is one 'of which the dames of a court might gladly have availed themselves, to add the richer and more spiritual adornment of human ingenuity to their fabrics of silk and gold' (p.74).

Body paragraph 2

Beautiful clothes are a mark of sin, evil and rebellion.

- **Hester:** Before we meet Hester or see her scarlet letter, a Puritan woman is already suggesting that her mark of shame can be covered up by 'a brooch, or suchlike heathenish adornment' (p.49). When we first see Hester and the letter, we learn that the letter is 'so artistically done, and with so much fertility and gorgeous luxuriance of fancy, that it had all the effect of a last and fitting decoration to the apparel which she wore; and which was of a splendor in accordance with the taste of the age, but greatly beyond what was allowed' (p.50) by the colony's rules. The women in the crowd notice it and it makes them angry (p.51). Hester has 'in her nature a rich, voluptuous, Oriental characteristic, – a taste for the gorgeously beautiful' (p.75). This taste, which aligns her with foreign, non-Christian and, therefore, morally suspect people, is expressed solely 'in the exquisite productions of her needle' (p.75).

- **Mistress Hibbins:** She is 'bitter-tempered' and will, sometime after the main events of the novel, be 'executed as a witch' (p.103). She keeps trying to recruit Hester (p.103) and Dimmesdale (p.193) to go to the forest to worship Satan. Her 'ruff' is 'done up with the famous yellow starch, of which Ann Turner, her especial friend, had taught her the secret' (p.193). Note 72 (p.237) tells us that this ruff-starching Ann Turner is a brothel-keeper and murderer. Regarding Mistress Hibbins, we read that as 'this ancient lady had the renown (which subsequently cost her no less a price than her life) of being a principal actor in all the works of necromancy that were continually going forward, the crowd ... seemed to fear the touch of her garment, as if it carried the plague among its gorgeous folds' (p.209).

- **Pearl:** We are reminded again and again that 'Her mother ... had bought the richest tissues that could be procured, and allowed her imaginative faculty its full play in the arrangement and decoration of the dresses which the child wore' (p.81). These clothes underscore Pearl's status as the living embodiment of the scarlet letter and they advertise to Governor Bellingham that 'we might have judged that such a child's mother must needs be a scarlet woman, and a worthy type of her of Babylon!' (p.98). When we see Pearl at play, we learn that she 'inherited her mother's gift for devising drapery and costume' (p.155). She uses this gift to imitate her mother's mark of sin, 'the letter A, – but freshly green, instead of scarlet!' (p.155) and to transform herself into non-human, non-Christian entities, such as a mermaid (p.155) and a fairy (p.180).

Body paragraph 3

Beautiful clothes are more commonly needed in this community than we might think. Most people need them at some time in their lives.

- Hester's rich needlework is in demand for 'the array of funerals' and for 'baby-linen – for babies then wore robes of state' (p.74), though she is not the seamstress of choice 'to embroider the white veil which was to cover the pure blushes of a bride' (p.75).

- Hawthorne refers to women in general, including Puritan women, as 'wearers of petticoat and farthingale' (p.48) – two types of basically unnecessary ornamental ladies' underclothing that historical Puritan women, especially of the lower social classes, probably didn't wear, but which Hawthorne implies that they do wear in his romance.

Sample conclusion

Hawthorne uses beautiful clothing in *The Scarlet Letter* to draw attention to the inextricable intertwining of wealth and high status with sin and evil. At the same time, by giving even ordinary people occasions on which to wear beautiful clothes, Hawthorne implies that sin and evil are inevitable aspects of every human life just as joy and virtue are. Moreover, near the novel's end, Hawthorne raises the question of whether ugly, plain clothing is just as much an affectation as beautiful clothing. On Election Day, 'as on all other occasions, for seven years past, Hester was clad in a garment of coarse gray cloth. Not more by its hue than by some indescribable peculiarity in its fashion, it had the effect of making her fade personally out of sight and outline' (p.197). This inconspicuous garment marks Hester as humble and penitent, but 'imparting so distinct a peculiarity to Hester's simple robe' is 'a task perhaps more difficult' (p.198) than creating Pearl's elaborate, showy gown. Beautiful clothes, Hawthorne has shown, are the vain trappings of sinful opulence. However, as the novel draws to its close, he implies that the self-consciously austere garments of pious Puritans may simply mark a different form of vanity.

SAMPLE ANSWER

What is the role of the forest in this novel and what is the role of the town?
The Scarlet Letter is set in seventeenth-century Boston, a small and
recently founded colonial town surrounded by a vast, wild forest. The
town is in the process of being created by a group of ardent Christians.
The forest is sparsely inhabited and the people who live there – Native
Americans – practise religions unfamiliar and unacceptable to the town-
dwellers. Sometimes the forest is represented as a beautiful, natural space
of permission, while the city is the dour, grim site of punishment. At other
times, the city is safe, civilised and familiar, while the forest is lonely,
eerie and terrifying. Each always represents the other's opposite. At the
same time, Hawthorne may be illustrating the consequences of rigidly
binary moralities (either/or, good/evil, black/white), such as those of the
Puritans, by representing the town and forest as necessary to each other,
with each being the other's dark reflection or evil twin.

The Scarlet Letter begins in the very centre of town, amidst a crowd
of people, at the scene of a public and spectacular punishment. Hester
Prynne, like 'a wild rose-bush'(p.45), is emerging from the iron-spike-
studded door of the 'gloomy' prison that is the necessary product of
'civilized society' (p.45). The townspeople are marked with a 'grim rigidity'
as they surround the town's central physical feature, 'the whipping-post'
(p.47). All this suggests that the town is a repressive and sadistic sphere,
yet the punished woman sees this town as her 'life-long home' (p.72), the
physical manifestation of 'the sphere of human charities' from which she
has been excluded (p.73). It is the physical manifestation of the religion
that has founded it and, as such, for its less liberal citizens, such as
Arthur Dimmesdale, Boston provides 'the pressure ... supporting, while
it confined him in its iron framework' (p.108). Outside it, 'the air was too
fresh and chill to be long breathed, with comfort' (p.109).

In contrast, the 'vast ... intricate and shadowy ... untamed' forest
around Boston is likened to 'a moral wilderness' (p.174). It is the 'dark,
inscrutable' (p.72) home of the fiendish, pagan Black Man; the site of the

satanic rituals to which Mistress Hibbins keeps inviting our protagonists (pp.103, 193) – Arthur Dimmesdale pictures her 'with some twigs of the forest clinging to her skirts' (p.133); and it is the sinister source from which Roger Chillingworth appears (pp.56, 65, 104). These details make the forest seem chaotic, dangerous and evil, yet it is also the home of dancing sunlight, Pearl's cute animal playmates and beautiful wildflowers. Its secluded, permissive space hosts Hester and Dimmesdale's joyous reunion (Chapters 17 and 18) and suggests itself as a possible refuge where Dimmesdale might 'hide [his] heart from the gaze of Roger Chillingworth' (p.172). When the town's morality is too strict, too painful, the forest offers a comforting, wild retreat whose very shifts in weather indicate its sympathy with the moods of the human heart.

In a moral system as rigid and binary as that of the Puritans, civilisation cannot exist without nature, nor good without evil. The Puritans' status as elect saints depends upon the status of non-Puritans as reprobate sinners; their heaven cannot exist without their hell. The outlaw Mistress Hibbins lives in the home of the lawmaker Governor Bellingham; Bostonian lawbreakers may be whipped at the town's centre or they may be 'driven with stripes into the shadow of the forest' (p.47) – freedom and imprisonment, virtue and punishment, are the two sides of a single coin. In *The Scarlet Letter*, the town represents civilisation and order, the forest represents nature and freedom – each with its attendant attractive and unattractive qualities. Each of these spaces is dependent upon the other to give it its character and meaning. It is crucial that the story moves back and forth between these two spheres. Our heroine, Hester, lives at the edge between the two, and her struggle reveals the possibilities and limitations of each. Through the drama of characters whose truths cannot be bound by civilisation's rules and yet cannot flourish in the lonely wilderness where no community exists, Hawthorne constructs a compelling argument for a more complex morality. Such a morality transcends the binaries of Puritanism and embraces both human singularity and human sympathy.

REFERENCES & READING

Text

Hawthorne, Nathaniel 2003, *The Scarlet Letter*, Penguin, New York (first published 1850).

Further reading

Baym, Nina 1986, *The Scarlet Letter: A Reading,* Twayne Publishers, Boston.

Colacurcio, Michael J. 1988, *New Essays on The Scarlet Letter*, Cambridge University Press, Cambridge.

Kennedy-Andrews, Elmer 1999, *Columbia Critical Guides: Nathaniel Hawthorne: The Scarlet Letter*, Columbia University Press, New York.

Scharnhorst, Gary 1992, *The Critical Response to Nathaniel Hawthorne's The Scarlet Letter*, Greenwood Press, New York.

notes

notes

notes

notes

notes

notes

notes

[2]

CPSIA information can be obtained at www.ICGtesting.com
Printed in the USA
LVOW071438231212

312975LV00002B/133/P

9 781921 411854